שִׁוִּיתִי יְיָ לְנֶגְדִּי תָמִיד

Na Nach Nachma Nachman Me'Uman

Prayers from the heart

- Rav Nathan of Breslev -

Vol.1

**In memory of
the chassidic Rabbi**

Rabbi Israel Dov Odeser ztk'l
Student of **Rabbi Israel Kardoner** ztk'l
Student of **Rabbi Moshe Breslover** ztk'l
Student of **Rabbi Natan of Breslov** ztk'l
Student of the holy master
**Rabbi Nachman of Breslov
Na Nach Nachma Nachman Me'Uman**
And In memory of the chassidic
Amram Yosef b'r Moshe Nahum Halevi **Horvitz** zt'l
Meir Akavya ben Ya'akov **Yemini** zt'l
Aharon Ben Ya'akov **Patz** zt'l

ת. נ. צ. ב. ה

Introduction

Rav Natan's Introduction

Rav Nachman cautioned us many times, in various ways, to make prayers out of the Torah discourses. He said that, from this act, great delight is created in Heaven and he said that no such delight has ever come before the Creator as the delight caused by these prayers made from Torah discourses. He spoke of this time and again with several different people.

However, he did not clarify fully what his holy intention was in this matter but we understood from his words that his main intention was simply that we try to delve into his holy, awesome Torah discourses which he revealed to us, to understand what he intended practically from each discourse. We should consider our ways (and perceive) how far away we are from the things mentioned in each discourse, then pray and plead to God, with many entreaties, requests and supplications, that He have mercy upon us and in His bountiful mercy, bring us closer to Him and that we merit to fulfill everything stated in that Torah discourse. Then we should pour out our hearts before the Holy One about all the things mentioned there, asking that we merit to fulfill them and ascertain them perfectly.

A person who merits to engage himself in making prayers from Torah discourses, as mentioned above,

Introduction

will always easily be able express himself before God and talk out everything that is in his heart by using each Torah discourse. Even though at first it may appear to him that this Torah does not speak about his own needs and about his own weaknesses and flaws, when he starts to talk using that discourse, God will certainly help him and he can put all he wants to say into it; everything that is on his heart, he can express by using each Torah; for the words of our Rebbe, may his memory be blessed, are very, very all-embracing. Each Torah discourse comprises the entire Torah and the generality of Israel and the generality of all things in the world. Each person, whoever he is, whether on the very highest spiritual level or whether on the lowest spiritual level, no matter what, from the top of all levels to the bottom of all levels, each one can find himself in all his aspects within each Torah discourse of our holy, awesome Rebbe, may his memory be blessed. Therefore, by each Torah discourse, every person in the world, at all times, can somehow express himself.

…Therefore, he who wants to have mercy on his soul and to really and truly consider his eternal purpose in life and who wants sincerely to come closer to the Holy One (should know) that it is well known and very clear that it is impossible to come closer to God, that is to say to break and nullify all the bad qualities and merit to all the good attributes and to progress in the pathway of God, other than by prayers, supplications, cries for help, imploring

Introduction

and shouting to God, for many days and years. All the tzaddikim and really kosher people merited to their spiritual levels only by this, by prayers and supplications as we have explained several times. However, to say many prayers and supplications is also very hard for a person because usually, one does not have the words to speak out and express oneself. By this method, mentioned above, of making prayers from Torah discourses, a person can easily express himself about everything that is in his heart, as explained previously. However, there are also many weighty obstacles against this also, for not every person is so familiar with the Rebbe's words such that he can make prayers from the Torah discourses, and so it is with other numerous obstacles. Therefore I made a point of copying from the prayers that I wrote for myself, as the Rebbe told me. He said that it is good to record for oneself the prayers when one merits to (compose) a well arranged prayer so that one can say it on another occasion. That is what I did. Afterwards I saw that it is good to copy them in a general language so that they will be equally valuable (useful) to each person and then to give them to our followers so as not to "withhold good from its owners," I saw that the (the prayers) are of great generality and that they (speak of) matters which each person needs, every single person according to his spiritual level. Everyone needs them, from the greatest to the smallest. There is nothing that a person lacks in the matter of serving God that will not be found in these prayers. When I copied some of them and gave them to a

Introduction

few people they liked them very, very much and pleaded with me to copy all of the prayers for them. Although I was uncertain in my heart about this, nevertheless I gave myself into the hands of the Holy One alone; I relied on Him alone. According to His good desire and the desire of our Rebbe, so will I do.

Any wise person, who really and purely wants to, will understand the virtue of these prayers. Prayers such as these have never existed in the world. They are full of good for the House of Israel – prayers, supplications, requests, entreaties, words of pardon and appeasement, confessions, claims, pretexts; great shouts, cries for help and imploring to God, to arouse His bountiful mercy upon us and asking that He bring us close to His service very quickly indeed. These prayers also contain great spiritual arousal that a person should use to speak to his soul, in order to awaken himself so that his life should not go by in a state of sleep, Heaven forbid. The power of speech has great power to arouse a person, therefore, when a person speaks out things, even though he knows them full well in his heart, he will arouse himself. By this he will strengthen himself, become full of determination and yearn even more to come closer to the Holy One, may His name be blessed, until he merits to really perfect repentance. A person who says these prayers regularly with truth and simplicity will certainly merit to the Eternal Life.

Introduction

It is good to do both things, 1) to engage oneself in meditation every day and speak to God about everything that is in one's heart, using one's mother tongue and 2) to make prayers out of Torah discourses, as mentioned previously. It is impossible to clarify in writing all the details about what a person needs, especially since all sorts of changes occur to a person all the time. The Rebbe, may his memory be blessed, warned us several times to say many supplications and requests every day, all sorts of supplications such as these which can be found in the big prayer-books, or the prayer-books Sha'arei Zion, or in other places. Even more so one should use the Book of Psalms. And he who wants to fulfill the Rebbe's holy words, to engage himself in saying prayers, to merit to the Eternal Life, his soul will certainly find these prayers very, very sweet (pleasurable) for there are no prayers in all the world in which a person can find himself such as these which talk of all sorts of virtue and all the things in the world, as a person can see for himself. Happy is the person who uses them.

May God hear our cries for help and hearken to our voices and to our prayers. May we merit constantly to engage ourselves in prayers and supplications, whether those written and arranged which are in our possession or whether those that a person has to speak out by himself from his heart in his own language every day, as our Rebbe warned us many times; for this is the main thing, as is clarified in his holy books many times.

Introduction

Through this, let us merit to really return to Him in complete repentance, as is His good desire, until we merit to rise up and be included in Him, in the light of the Ein Sof and "to behold the beauty of the Lord and visit His Temple" . In the merit of our prayers, bring us our righteous Meshiach very speedily, in our days; for the principal weapon of the Meshiach is prayer, as is explained in the Torah discourse 'Emor' – "Say to the Priests" – . One needs to strengthen oneself very much in the matter of prayers and supplications, no matter what happens, until God looks down and sees from Heaven. "After two days He will revive us: on the third day He will raise up and we shall live in His sight" that we "may walk before God in the light of the living" .
Amen and Amen.

The one who waits for salvation, Rav Natan, son of Rav Naftali Hertz, Nemirov, son-in-law if the famous Rav, Gaon David Zvi.

Table of contents

In this edition, each prayer number corresponds directly to the chapter number in Likutei Moharan.

Subject	Prayer No.
Advice	140, 143, 169
Anger	99, 119, 154
Brit - The Covenant	83, 130, 141, 169, 177
Calmness of Mind	78, 179
Children	151
Clothes	127-128
Confession	178, 179
Controversy and Strife	75, 95, 136, 179
Death	117, 144-145, 151
Desire and Yearning	92, 109, 142, 144-145, 154, 166-167, 177, 179
Eating	125-126, 177
Enthusiasm and Fervour	156
Eyes	93, 127-128, 133
Faith	91, 93, 108, 123, 129, 152, 154, 164, 173
Fear of God	108, 110, 135, 146, 148
Happiness and Sadness	169, 178, 179
Healing	179
Honour	168, 172

Table of contents

Subject	Prayer No.

Humility 130, 135, 147, 148, 168

Land of Israel 129, 154

Life and Longevity 109, 144-145, 157, 159, 179

Love 75, 93, 101, 115, 135, 165, 178, 179

Meditation 108, 122, 178

Melody and Song 142, 149

Merit in Others 178

Messiah 118, 178

Midnight Prayer 149

Money 80, 143, 153, 154, 159, 180

Overcoming Obstacles 115, 142, 147, 149, 154, 178, 179

Peace 75, 95, 136, 179

Physical Desires 75, 78, 101, 133, 144, 146, 157, 160, 179

Praise 99, 125-126, 142, 178

Prayers 97, 99, 122, 154, 179

Purity and Holiness of Heart 92, 108, 123, 137-138, 141, 156, 157, 165, 176

Repentance 105, 109, 135, 179

Shabbat and Festivals 117, 119, 125-126, 166-167, 135

Shame 97, 108, 146, 147, 179

Simplicity 123, 154

Sleep 149

Table of contents

Subject	Prayer No.
Suffering	106, 165, 170, 180
Controlling Thoughts	91, 97, 130, 133
Torah	75, 78, 92, 99, 101, 105, 110, 118, 133, 142, 146, 154, 157, 159, 164, 173
Travelling	154
Trust in God	99, 159
Truth	115, 122, 123, 136, 171
Tzaddik	91, 92, 110, 120, 123, 125, 129, 133, 135, 140, 143, 152, 153, 166, 176
Understanding	91, 99, 101, 105, 106, 117, 171
Weddings	178

Prayers from the heart

Prayer 75

Master of the World, merit me to the attribute of peace. Let me be a lover of peace and to always pursue peace. Guard me and save me through Your immense compassion from the trait of wanting to triumph over others and from controversy stemming from the other side. Let my heart be free from these traits which come from blood in the body which has not been used to serve the Holy One. Have mercy upon me and merit me from now on to study Torah and pray a lot. May I speak out many words of Torah and prayer every single day until I use every drop of blood in me to service God. May all the drops of blood within me become holy words of Torah and prayer until no drop of blood remains that has not served the Holy One.

Father, merit me to serve You with all my strength throughout my lifetime with every drop of blood that I have. Let me verbalize so many words of Torah and prayer that my body becomes completely negated as if it is actually nothing at all. Please merit me to perfect fear before You at all times. Draw down and bestow in my heart fear, shame, dread and a great awe before You constantly.

Through this, merit me to clarify, elevate and purify all the letters and sparks that fell into the world, as 'broken vessels'. As a result of my sins and enormous iniquities, in this lifetime and in previous lifetimes. These sins lead to controversy, doubts, confusion and obstacles to Your holy service and from these stem all the physical cravings in the world. May I have the strength to elevate all the fallen sparks to You. As a result, may the Holy One and the Shechinah be united and through this, may a great and wonderful peace exist in the World Above and Below and in all the worlds. Let there be great love and peace between all the Jewish people and all created things in the world.

Prayer 78

May it be Your will God our God and God of our Fathers that in Your great compassion You help me and merit me to sanctify the words of my mouth always. May I say holy words every day constantly and pray a lot. Protect us and guard us so that no word escapes our lips

Prayers from the Heart / Prayer 78

that is not according to Your will. May we never blemish our speech. Rather, merit us to sanctify our speech at all times and to speak abundantly, words of Torah, prayer and other holy words.

My Father, compassionate Father, bring me close to Your holy Torah. Merit me to study and contemplate You Torah day and night until I merit to cool down all the heat of my passion by means of my words of Torah and prayer. For You know the degree to which my heart burns with flames of fire; Sometimes my heart burns exceedingly to you as a furnace, but out of control, until my body could be burnt up God forbid and in the middle of this my mind becomes confused and my heart changes and burns God forbid to the physical cravings as a torch of fire, like a burning oven which wants to burn up my body and soul, Heaven forbid.

Now I have no wisdom or advice other than to shout out to You until You bring me closer to You for Your sake out of Your bountiful compassion. Hover over me and protect me. Save me. Blow on my heart so that this will put out the fire of my evil cravings. Drive out from me the spirit of folly. Merit me to draw upon myself the spirit of life, the spirit of holiness. May I fulfill the verse which says: "Let the Book of Torah not cease from your lips and you will study it by day and by night".

Prayers from the Heart / Prayer 80

And merit us to recognize You truly above and beyond all the worlds.

Prayer 80

Help me and bring me salvation so that I am always ready to really sacrifice my soul to sanctify Your Name, especially at the time of reciting "Shma Yisrael" and praying. Merit me to fix in my mind very firmly, with a strong desire, readiness to sacrifice my soul to sanctify Your name while burning with enthusiasm so that I can overpower my evil urge and thus give over all my body, soul and all my money in order to sanctify Your holy Name. May I, by this, be able to always pray with great concentration in true holiness and purity. And let me put all my mind and thoughts into the words of prayer, connecting my thoughts to the words very firmly indeed.

As a result please find pleasure in my prayers.

God, I need many wonderful forms of salvations all the time. In Your bountiful compassion open up Your fountains of salvation. May the salvation flow and renew itself all the time at every moment in such a manner that we are saved from what we need to be saved from. Sanctify and purify us, through these streams of salvation, from all the impurities, stains and blemishes in the world. Fulfill in us the verse which says: "And I will throw over You, pure waters and will You will be purified; from all the impurities and all the idols I will purify You".

Master of the World who makes salvations flourish. Fulfill our wishes for our good. Save us hastily and bring us salvation both materially and spiritually in whatever we need. And let this be in such a manner that I return to You and come closer to You in truth.

Prayer 83

Master of the World. Merit me to guard the brit perfectly. May I sanctify myself even in what is permissible such that my marital relations will be an aspect of "if meritorious the Shechinah dwells between them." You informed us that by blemishing the brit, by a nocturnal emission, one causes a strengthening of the harsh decrees and of God's wrath in the world, Heaven forbid. This is an aspect of "if not meritorious, fire devours them". Therefore let us give charity to worthy poor people especially in an anonymous manner and by this my all the harsh decrees which were created by a blemishing of the brit be sweetened. Fulfill in us the verse "Anonymous charity subdues the wrath". Merit us from now on to be saved from all kinds of blemishes of the brit.

Prayer 91

All Your commandments are faith. God of faith have compassion over me for Your sake. Merit me to real faith. Help me and save me so that I strengthen myself with perfect faith constantly. Merit me to achieve higher and higher levels of faith until I reach, understand and ascertain in my mind things that I was unable to understand previously. Enable me to acquire complete faith so that it spreads through all my limbs. Master of the World grant me faith. Master of the World, You know everything that happens in the world with regards to the holy faith which is the foundation of everything especially what the Jewish People, Your holy nation are going through, who are believers, the descendants of believers. Even so there are thousands and tens of thousands of levels in faith and all the troubles and exiles that the Jewish People experience are because of blemishes in faith for it is the basis of all Torah as the holy Sages have revealed to us.

Master of the World, merciful One. How can we rectify this? From where should we start to rectify it?

Prayers from the Heart / Prayer 91

In Your bountiful mercy, You sent us true holy and awesome tzaddikim in each generation who revealed to us wonderful and sublime Torah innovations. They draw down and teach holy belief, eye to eye, to all people. But even after all this we have not retracted from our mistakes and this has caused us all the troubles that befall us. We are in great distress, both generally and individually.

God of faith, have mercy on us. Save us. Hear my prayers. Listen to my pleading. In Your righteousness, answer me. Help me for Your Name's sake.

Strengthen me to know and believe in You every moment in such a way that I will be saved by this from all kinds of sins, iniquities and willful sins, from all kinds of bad thoughts and all sorts of confusions, especially crookedness of the heart and thoughts against Your holy faith. Teach us to draw upon ourselves holy faith which our Fathers, Sages and tzaddikim achieved through their immense holiness. Merit us to draw upon ourselves their faith and their kindness and their goodness and their righteousness for which they struggled and toiled with self-sacrifice to bestow goodness upon all the people of Israel, the Jewish People, for all generations; and the main thing (they toiled for, was) to draw down and reveal the holy belief to the whole world in general and especially the holy People of Israel, The Jewish People, the nation near to Him, His treasured nation. Help us and save us at this time of trouble for the sake of their strength and their unfathomably great and awesome merit. Save us God, for the waters have risen to drown me. Merit us to complete faith in truth until I merit each time, through the holy faith to come to understanding and the holy faith spreads over all of us and into each and every one of our limbs. Merit us always to talk about the holy faith openly with our mouths, wholeheartedly and in truth as it is written in Psalms "I will always sing the kindnesses of God, from generation to generation I will make known your faithfulness with my mouth" and it is written there "and the heavens will acknowledge you wonders O Lord; your faithfulness too, in the congregation of the holy" and it is written in Psalms "Your faithfulness lasts throughout the generations. You have established the earth, and it stands" and it is written there "I have chosen the way of faith. I have put your laws (before me)" and it is written (Psalms) "for God's word (i.e. His judgment and decrees) is upright and all His deeds are in good faith" and it says in the book of Chavakuk "the righteous man who lives by his faith" and in Psalms it says "my faithfulness and loving kindness will be with him and his horn will be exalted through My Name" and it says there "for God is good. His kindness is everlasting, and his faithfulness (to keep His promise) is throughout the generations" and the Prphet Hoshaya says "I will make you my bride forever. I will make you my bride (in reward for your) righteousness and justice and kindness and compassion. I will make you my bride (in reward for your) faith. Then you will know God". Blessed are you Lord forever and ever Amen. Amen.

Prayer 92

Master of the World, You informed us of the greatness of the holy tzaddikim who have the power to revive the dead by walking back and forth in their house. By this they sweeten all the harsh decrees. Have mercy on us and let us come close to tzaddikim like these. Merit me to engage myself in studying Your holy Torah every single day so that I can cool down the fire which burns in my heart for all the cravings and vanities of this world. Rather, may my heart burn with great holiness, yearning to Your Torah and Your service in the proper measure. Let me cleave to Your Torah, so much that I become merged with it in Your Oneness and let me be numbered among the holy tzaddikim. And by walking back and forth in my house enable me to sweeten all the harsh decrees and draw down an aspect of the revival of the dead.

Prayer 93

Master of the World, merit us to perform the mitzvah of "And you shall love the Lord your God with all your heart" which is the source of all the mitzvot. May I engage in studying Torah a lot and serve Torah scholars. Merit me to carry out business affairs with faith such that the Name of Heaven becomes loved through me. By this, enable me to reach a spiritual level which is above time and to achieve expanded consciousness. As a result, merit me to pray with great concentration and a pure mind.

Merit me to holy eyes and a pure and very clear power of vision such that through this alone I will be able to look at something with wisdom and intelligence and with perfect faith. Let me believe that in each object there are letters and holy sparks. By this looking, may all the sparks rise that are clothed in the object so they return to their source in the aspect of "Engraved like a signet ring, Holy to God." And from the letters and sparks may words be made and by these holy words bestow much good to the House of Israel for this is Your main delight, so to speak.

Prayers from the Heart / Prayer 95

Have mercy on all the letters and holy sparks which are in a deep exile and speedily redeem them for Your Name's sake until Your glory is lifted up and exalted.

Prayer 95

You, Who makes peace in the heavens, bring peace upon us and all the Jewish People. Master of the World. Save me from all forms of controversy and from being abused and attacked. Help me to avoid feeling proud; may I never have a sense of pride in relation to any other person.

Help all the benefactors and leaders of the generation to avoid pride, Heaven forbid. Don't let them be haughty. Rather may they consider themselves to be an aspect of "what" - non-existent and nothing. By this, save them from all kinds of controversy and insults and arrange for us benefactors and leaders who are pious and honest.

Prayer 97

Master of the World, You know how far I am from proper prayer and supplications. The main reason is because of thoughts that bother me, both before and during the prayers. Thoughts of self importance and ulterior motives and many extraneous, bad thoughts and confusions. They are endless and innumerable. There are many prayers that are so mixed up with these thoughts that I was unaware that I had recited words of prayer. Many words of prayer and blessings I just skipped over completely without noticing. What I recited is as if I had said nothing, for the words were far away from my heart. My heart was full of bad, extraneous and confused thoughts. Where will I hide and conceal myself in the face of my great shame and disgrace which is so immense and bitter? The mouth cannot describe it nor the heart imagine it.

I have come before You, Who listens to prayer and chooses the prayers of the Jewish nation out of compassion. You long for the prayers of Jews. For this, You created the world. So, help us at all times to drive out these thoughts which bother and confuse us and merit us to pray before You with all our heart, with great concentration from the depths of our heart truly. May our thoughts be holy and pure so that our thoughts will be connected firmly to the words of prayer, with total unity. At the time of prayer let no ulterior intention or extraneous thought enter my heart, rather merit us to remove all these thoughts and the foolish vain ideas of self importance. Help me to forget about any importance stemming from the status of my family and may I never imagine that I have already struggled and achieved a lot in the service of God. Rather, let me truly recognize my deficiencies and my lowly status so that I will not have any thoughts of pride or superiority.

Grant the power to rule in our prayers such that we have the power to bring about what we want through our prayers, even to alter nature. Fulfill the wishes of our heart for the good out of Your mercy. Take delight in our prayers always. Draw upon us Your loving-kindness at all times; sweeten and nullify from upon us and upon all of the Jewish People, all the harsh decrees in the world. Break and nullify all the harsh decrees whether those that have already been decreed or whether those that they want to decree, Heaven forbid.

Master of the World, merciful One. Help us, like You did for our Fathers. Protect and save us in every generation. See our weakness and fight our battle (with the evil urge). Redeem us speedily, a full redemption, for Your Name's sake.

Prayer 99

Lord, open my lips and let my mouth speak Your praises. Master of the World, merit me to pray before You with great concentration and tremendous devotion. Let my prayer be smooth and fluent in my mouth. Even when I do not manage to pray with real devotion as I should, nevertheless, merit me to put all my strength, concentration and heart into the words of prayer with maximum focus. May I truly believe and put my trust in Your great loving kindness. And when You help me to pray before You with great devotion, as is fitting, and my prayer is fluent, then may all the other prayers rise up together with this one that I merited to pray properly. By this, enable me to always strengthen myself in the service of prayer. Fulfill the verse which says: "May my prayer come before You; give your ear to my song".

Master of the World, merit me to engage myself in studying Torah a lot. Enlighten our eyes in Your Torah. Help me to ascertain the great light from the radiance of the Torah. However, as I ascertain more each time in the understanding of the holy Torah, so merit me to add righteousness, piety and good deeds. By this, may I be pleased with others without showing any anger or strictness towards anyone at all. Rather let me be good to everyone. Even if I show to one individual some displeasure about something I consider to be improper, nevertheless let me speak to him positively and softly so that my words will be acceptable and settle in his heart. Fulfill in me the verse: "The words of Torah scholars are calm." "Let me find favour and good understanding in the eyes of God and of people".

Prayer 101

Master of the World, unique Lord, Who gives the Torah. You revealed to us that all the strength of the other nations is from the Seventy Faces of Darkness. That is to say, by our being lax in studying Torah and not studying in depth as we should, as a result, the paths of Torah are blocked and become darkened in our eyes. Then, all the physical cravings and bad traits overcome us Heaven save us, for they stem from the other nations whose strength is drawn from the Faces of Darkness. This itself leads to the governments becoming more forceful, Heaven forbid and they decree harsh judgments upon us, Heaven save us. But what can we do to rectify this. The burden of making a living, the strength of the evil urge and the many troubles make it hard for us to study properly. Even the little we study,

Prayers from the Heart / Prayer 101

the darkness in our eyes and our blocked minds prevent us from studying or understanding properly. Mostly, we do not understand even the simple meaning of things. We certainly do not understand the depth of things, not the pleasantness, inner essence or secrets of the Torah. For we do not merit to see the light of the face of the holy Torah. We are far, far away for the Seventy Faces of the Torah, from the Seventy Faces of Light which subdue the Seventy Faces of Darkness. When they are subdued, automatically the governments of the seventy nations, whose strength comes from those Seventy Faces of Darkness, are broken and fall. But how do we merit to this. In Your bountiful compassion, have mercy on us and grant us a portion in Your Torah. Merit us from now on to be aroused to serve You. Let us start from now on to study Torah by day and by night. Do not let the burden of making a living disturb us, rather let others work for us. As a result, may our main involvement be studying the Torah in this world and may it accompany us to the World to Come.

In Your immense bountiful mercy, enlighten our eyes in Your Torah and open up our hearts so that we merit to understand well and with great speed any part of the Torah we study. Let us study all the books of Your Torah every day, Tanach, Talmud, Halacha, Midrashim, the holy Zohar and the Tikkunim, all the writings of the Ariz"l and those of the true tzaddikim. May we finish them and then study them again and again during our lifetime. Have mercy on us for Your Name's sake and merit us to study consistently with holiness and persistence by day and by night. By this, may we break, nullify and kill all the evil cravings and all the evil traits in our body.

Merciful One, grant us intelligence and understanding to hear, study and teach, keep and perform all the words of Your Torah, with love. Merit us to put all our mind and thoughts into Your holy Torah at all times in such a way that the Torah will shine upon us the holy pleasantness of the light of its face. May it radiate upon us and protect us through all of the Seventy Faces of the Torah which the true tzaddikim merited to ascertain. As a result, enable us to break and nullify all the physical cravings and bad traits from within us.

In these troubled times have mercy on us, do it for Your sake, for the Sake of our Fathers and for the sake of all the holy and awesome tzaddikim who were in each generation. Then speedily break and nullify all the harsh decrees from upon us, whether those that have already been decreed or whether those that they want to decree against us Heaven forbid. Let no impression of them remain at all. May the words of my mouth and the meditation of my heart be pleasing before Your countenance, God, my Rock and my Redeemer. Amen.

Prayer 105

May it be Your will, God, our God, God of our Fathers, have mercy upon us. Help us to merit to engage ourselves in studying Your Holy Torah. May the words of Torah never cease from my mouth and the mouths of our children, forever. Merit us to understand completely all the words of Your holy Torah with great speed. Then let us understand one thing from another and create true Torah innovations, innovations that will find favour before Your Throne of Glory. By studying Torah may we achieve full repentance for all our sins, iniquities and willful sins that we have committed over the years. Let the light of the Torah really return us to the path of goodness and through studying Torah may we separate, collect and raise up all the holy sparks and combinations of letters that have fallen from all the worlds into the husks because of us. They have scattered to where they have scattered and fallen where they have fallen.

Have mercy upon us, upon all the holy sparks and upon all the holy letters which are separated and scattered among the nations and among the husks. Help us to return in true repentance to You. Please hasten to clarify, collect and redeem all the holy sparks from their exile.

Prayers from the Heart / Prayer 106

Return them to their place in peace and by this, rectify the blemish of the worlds.

Draw holy understanding and great mercy in the world. Nullify anger and cruelty from the world. Please, You Yourself, pray on our behalf. By Your simple mercy, arouse Your great plentiful mercy. You know Lord our God, that none can stand up for us other than You. Our Father, our King, pray for us. We have no one to rely on other than our Father in Heaven, so have mercy and compassion upon us. Save us for Your Name's Sake. May the words of my mouth and the meditation of my heart be pleasing before Your Countenance, oh God, my Rock and my Redeemer.

Prayer 106

You endow man with knowledge and teach understanding. Grant us wisdom, insight and knowledge for You know how greatly a person needs mercy if he lacks knowledge in the service of God. You also informed us how all the harsh decrees and suffering, Heaven save us, are drawn upon us only because of brains of limited perception. Therefore, have mercy on us, and in Your bountiful compassion, merit us to strengthen ourselves each time and rise from these 'small brains' to 'expansive brains' of understanding. Bestow upon us a bounty of knowledge and wisdom. Merit us also to give intelligence to others so that they will also have a radiance of true knowledge, thus raising me from the aspect of 'small brains' to 'expansive brains'. By this alone may my own brains be aroused. Then sweeten and nullify from upon us and all the Jewish People, all the harsh decrees. Fulfill in us the verse: 'Draw Your loving-kindness to those who know You'.

Prayer 108

Master of the World, merciful One, Who cures those with broken hearts, You know my broken and depressed heart. Have mercy on my broken heart for it is broken to smithereens; for the thoughts of my heart are scattered and dispersed to the ends of the earth. I am really responsible for all this but I did not have bad intentions.

Master of the World, You know the hidden secrets of the world, You see into the chambers of our hearts. Before You, all the hidden thoughts of the heart are revealed. You know how hard this itself is for me; it confuses and obstructs me a lot. Even if sometimes in Your great compassion You send me some words and I begin to explain to You all that is in my heart, after a while my heart becomes blocked in the middle of speaking. So also my heart suddenly becomes sealed. I do not know what to do. You seem to hide Your face from me. You have already revealed to us that this is caused by us blemishing our faith for this is considered to be like idol worship. Now, my Father in Heaven, what can I do to atone for this? Oh, what can I do to return Your face towards me. When will I merit to pure faith so that I can speak openly before You, as if face to face, like one speaks to a friend.

Help me and save me so that I can accustom myself to sigh, deep sighs from the depths of the heart about my vast distance from You because of my many sins, especially blemishes to faith. Merit me to truly feel my pain and immense suffering such that I really sigh from the depths of my heart. May my spirit be broken within me in a way that will arouse Your true compassion upon me. Open Your hand in mercy and good will and bring me back to You in repentance face to face. Father in Heaven, faithful King, God of faith, You know everything that happens to us and to every individual regarding holy faith. In You great compassion, You planted Your faith within us, but because of the immense number of our sins we still get thoughts of blasphemy. This is the main cause of our distance from You. It causes a concealment

Prayers from the Heart / Prayer 108

of Your face, which is the greatest of all our troubles and distress.

Guard us and protect us from now on from all sorts of disbelief and blasphemous thoughts. Rather, merit me to believe in You Lord our God, in Your Holy Torah and in Your tzaddikim with total faith, a faith that is pure and perfect. May my faith be so strong that it is as if I see You, eye to eye. By this, may fear of You be on my face; let me feel shame, so that I will never sin again nor blemish in any way. Let awe, dread and fear of You, with great shame, descend upon me immediately knowing that You stand over me, and see my every deed, at all times and at every moment. And merit me, through the strength of my holy belief, to pray, plead and speak openly before You with all my heart and with proper thoughts. Let my mind be connected firmly to the words of prayer without any extraneous thoughts and may all my words and conversations with You be as if face to face, like someone speaking to his friend.

Have mercy upon me like a father over his son. Save me on every occasion by all kinds of salvation. May You be blessed forever. Amen and Amen.

Prayer 109

O Lord, our God and God of our fathers. Please help me to return in really perfect repentance before You. Master of the World. You know how greatly I have distanced myself from You because of many and immense iniquities and willful transgressions which reach to the Heavens. I do not know any way to return to You. My mind has become very confused, befouled and materialized because of the material and foul matter and evil cravings that have taken hold of me and attached themselves to me very much. Master of all the World, take pity and have mercy upon me; grant me good advice, how to look for, search out and find some road, course or pathway, such that from now on I can merit to return to You. In Your bountiful mercy, let me merit to often sigh before You from the depths of my heart about my great distance from You. Let me merit to really come closer to You. May I really sigh about this at all times such that my body be broken by each and every sigh. By these sighs, let me merit to extract the spirit and air of the Other Side and to plant within me the spirit and air of holiness. Through this, may I uproot and cut the cord of impurity which has become tied to me because of my many iniquities. Help me, very speedily, to cut

Prayers from the Heart / Prayer 109

and break myself completely from the cord of impurity. Let me cleave and tie myself, in a very strong bond, to the cord of holiness, for ever and ever, for all eternities. Break, drive out and nullify from me, from my body, my soul, my spirit and my higher soul, all sorts of impurities of the Other Side. In Your mercy, bring me close to the cord of holiness and tie me to it with a strong and firm knot from now on, forever.

From now on, draw upon me a good long life, by way of the cord of holiness. Be gracious and bestow upon us good bounty, blessings, compassion, life, peace and plenty; real life; life of holiness, life that has fear of Heaven; life in which we merit to really perfect repentance, in which we always serve You and cleave to the Source of Life. Living God, our Portion in Life, our Rock, give us life in the light of Your Countenance; raise me up so that I live a life of holiness. Take pity on me, help me and make my heart cleave to Your commandments. Let me merit to always cleave to You forever more. In Your mercy protect me and save me from sighs of the Other Side. Let no breath or sigh for the cravings and vanities of This World leave my mouth. Heaven forbid. Rather, may all my sighs, yearnings and desires be only for Your Name, for Your worship, to really come closer to You. May I always cleave to You and may it be fulfilled in me the verse which says: "You who cleave to the Lord, your God, are all alive this day". Amen and Amen.

Prayer 110

Please God, save me in Your bountiful mercy, so that I merit to engage in studying Torah for its own sake, with great consistency and perseverance, by day and by night. Be with me always to assist and save me so that I will not materialize or darken the words of Torah in my mouth, Heaven forbid. Rather, merit me to study Torah with great holiness and purity, nullifying myself and all my materiality at the time of studying. By this let me feel in my heart and mind the sweetness and pleasantness of the spirituality of the mind. Rather, merit me to pure thoughts, holy thoughts which are really bright and proper.

Let me constantly serve You with true Fear of Heaven and wholeheartedly. Enable me to come close to genuine tzaddikim and to pure, straightforward Jews until they bring me into the realm of holiness and genuine repentance.

Prayer 115

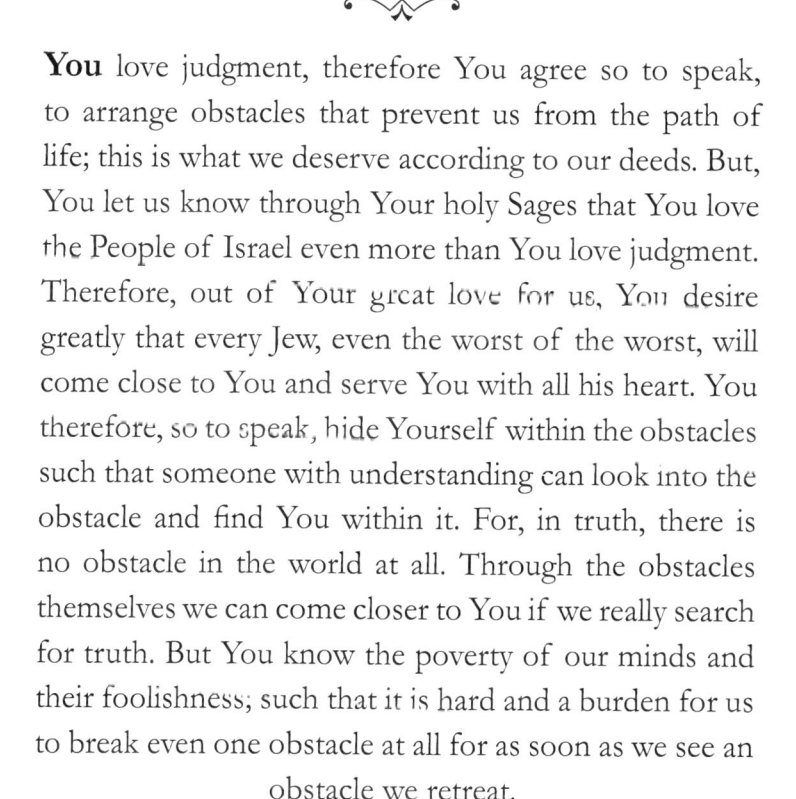

You love judgment, therefore You agree so to speak, to arrange obstacles that prevent us from the path of life; this is what we deserve according to our deeds. But, You let us know through Your holy Sages that You love the People of Israel even more than You love judgment. Therefore, out of Your great love for us, You desire greatly that every Jew, even the worst of the worst, will come close to You and serve You with all his heart. You therefore, so to speak, hide Yourself within the obstacles such that someone with understanding can look into the obstacle and find You within it. For, in truth, there is no obstacle in the world at all. Through the obstacles themselves we can come closer to You if we really search for truth. But You know the poverty of our minds and their foolishness; such that it is hard and a burden for us to break even one obstacle at all for as soon as we see an obstacle we retreat.

Therefore, please bring us closer to You in charity and as a gift out of loving kindness. Give us the strength to break all the obstacles that come from the aspect of harsh decrees and judgment. Sweeten and nullify all the harsh decrees from upon us and from all of the Jewish People. Do not let any obstacle prevent us from now on from truly coming close to You. Act charitably to us in judgment. Blessed are You, oh King who loves charity and judgment.

Prayer 116

Master of the World, merit me to give away a lot of charity to deserving poor people. Make us feel in our heart mercy towards poor people and merit us to bestow upon them great loving kindness. By this, have mercy upon us, as the Sages said: 'Anyone who has mercy on others, from Heaven they have mercy on him'.

Save us from all kinds of spirit of folly and by this, protect us from coming to any form of sin. Merit us to perform Your will all the days of our life. Amen.

Prayer 117

You informed us that every motzei Shabbat an aspect of the revelation of Eliyahu the Prophet begins. Therefore, have mercy upon us and merit us to receive the holiness of Shabbat properly. By this, merit us immediately after Shabbat ends to receive a true radiance of the revelation of the prophet. Merit us to perform the mitzvah of

Havdala over wine every motzei Shabbat. As a result, enable us to receive radiance of true, holy understanding such that we merit to serve You with full understanding all through the week. Help us to distance all falsehood which stems from an aspect of the serpent who brought death to the world. Merit us to cleave to the attribute of truth which is an aspect of the elixir of life. So may it be Your will. Amen.

Prayer 118

Master of the World, who gives the Torah, have mercy upon us and let us merit to engage ourselves in learning Your holy Torah for its own sake, with great diligence and perseverance. Grant us merit to learn a great deal every day. Help us so that every holy book that we learn, we be able to explain well, in a way that we understand. Let this be in such a way that we merit to arouse and draw upon ourselves the spirit of Messiah which is "the spirit of God that hovers over the waters", waters which represent the Torah. Messiah suffers many illnesses and is afflicted with great suffering because of our willful transgressions and iniquities, this being in order to atone for us and to save us from all the troubles. By this he gives us a chance to survive. Have mercy upon him and

Prayers from the Heart / Prayer 118

upon us and let us merit to engage ourselves a great deal in learning Torah. Let us explain well each thing that we learn in a language that is understood, especially when learning with friends or with students, such that our words enter their ears and hearts. By this, let the spirit of Messiah be aroused upon us. He suffers greatly for us. He lowers himself and dresses himself in many common, everyday appearances in order to be with us, in order to revive us and establish us in the midst of this long, powerful and bitter exile.

Our Father, merciful Father, have mercy upon us, help us and save us, in his merit, in his strength. Save us from all the troubles and from all the harsh decrees, whether those that have already been passed against us or those that they wait to decree. Heaven forbid, for the "power of endurance fails." Rock of Israel, rise and come to the assistance of Israel. Speedily save us in these troubled times through the strength and merit of our righteous Messiah, the holy one of Israel. Fulfill in us the verse which says: "Now I know that he Lord saves His anointed (Messiah); He will hear him from His holy heaven with the saving strength of His right hand". And it says, "Great deliverance He gives to His king and shows loving-kindness to His Messiah, to David and to his seed forever." And it says, "The Lord is their strength and He is the saving strength of His Messiah." Save us

Lord: let the King hear us when we call." Amen and Amen.

Prayer 119

You grant knowledge to man. Please bestow upon us wisdom, insight and knowledge. Through this merit us to cleave to the attribute of compassion so that we have compassion on others. Save us from all kinds of anger and cruelty which stem from foolishness and a lack of knowledge. Rather enable us to overcome this and listen to ourselves each time to behave with compassion. As a result please have mercy upon us from Heaven as the Sages said: "Anyone who has compassion over others, they have compassion on him from Heaven".

You know how much we need a salvation and mercy from Heaven, each person in his own way. Only You know all the difficult experiences both spiritually and materially that occur to us nowadays in general and individually. You who know how great our weakness is and the deficiencies of our knowledge. As a result we do not have the power to arouse Your compassion over us in a complete way. 'delete'

You revealed to us that the holy Shabbat is an aspect of knowledge for on Shabbat each Jew draws upon himself holy knowledge. Therefore, please have mercy upon us and merit us to receive Shabbat properly such that through this we will be able to receive the light of knowledge. As a result, let us ascertain the attribute of compassion and have mercy on other Jews, so that I can do good for them, as is fitting. Save me from all sorts of anger; sweeten and nullify all the harsh decrees from upon us and from upon all the Jewish People. Amen. May it be so.

Prayer 120 – 121

Master of the Universe, grant me the merit to come close to true tzaddikim and to hear words of Torah and inspiration from their mouths so that I will receive real spiritual arousal in the service of God with fear of Heaven. You know that I have already looked into a number of holy books of ethics but I still have not really been inspired by them. This is because books are on the level of 'action' and after the sin of the golden calf we lost the crown of 'action'. So merit me to hear words of Torah and inspiration with my own ears from the mouth of the tzaddik for this is an aspect of 'listening' and 'Comprehending'. If we hear directly from him this will have more power to arouse us to truly repent.

Prayers from the Heart / Prayer 122

So merit me to yearn and long so much to serve You with great desire that in any book I learn from I will immediately find myself. In other words let me see my own worthlessness and lowly spiritual status. As a result may I get great spiritual arousal and inspiration to serve You from each and every holy book that I study. May I receive from them good advice, inspiration and tremendous encouragement in Your service. Fulfill in me the verse: "Then I said, behold I have come with the scroll of the book that is written for me specifically". May I consider everything I learn from a book of God to have been written "for me" as if it is speaks to me personally, telling me to perform Your will. Amen. So may it be Your will.

Prayer 122

Save me from the trait of wanting to triumph over others. Let me feel more comfortable to be vanquished than to win. For You know how very many people have lost their world completely Heaven save us, through this trait of being wanting to be a winner, for triumph does not allow for truth. Even if a person sees with his own eyes that something is true, he will reject it for the sake of triumphing. Merit me to cleave to the attribute of truth and to always admit the truth. Let me always speak the truth for specifically by this, I will eventually merit to vanquish all those who oppose me and try to distance me from the path of truth. Protect me so that I do not mislead myself through the trait of wanting to vanquish others.

You taught us that You yearn and long for the Jewish People to triumph over You in their prayers such that You change Your will, so to speak, to our will. You take great delight when we triumph over You. And how could we do this other than by You sending us the words and claims by which to vanquish You.

So have mercy on me and send me words in order to explain myself before You at all times with new and proper claims, requests, supplications and appeasements until I vanquish You so to speak. As a result, bring me close to You, even though I am not deserving, for Your compassion is immense Amen, so may it be Your will.

Prayer 123

"**Fortunate** are those whose path is simplicity, who walk in the Torah of the Lord. I will behave wisely in a perfect, pure way. When will You come to me? I will walk with a pure heart within my house. Let (my deeds of) purity and integrity protect me. I hope and wait for You. As for me I will walk in my purity; redeem me and be merciful upon me".

Master of the World, full of mercy, whose deeds are perfect and who is pure and shows His purity with the pure. Have mercy upon me and let me merit to real purity and simplicity May I merit to really attach myself in purity and simplicity to the real tzaddikim, the pious and pure people in the generation who merited to serve real tzaddikim and to receive from them the path of truth and honesty. Grant me the merit to discard, remove and nullify all my wisdom, intellect and perception before them such that it is as if I have no intellect at all. Let me fulfill all that they say and anything they say let that be it! Let me not stray to the right or the left of what they say. Master of the Compassion, have mercy upon me and save me from all sorts of confusions, from all sorts of worldly wisdoms that are not true. Have mercy upon me and save me from them. Do not let my heart be delivered into their ways. Let me not stray from the words of the truly holy tzaddikim who lead us in mercy, in truth and purity according to the ways of the Torah that we received from the mouth of our teacher, Moses, may he rest in peace. Protect us and save us from all sorts of denial of faith and things that confuse our faith, which are the result of these alien wisdoms. Let me merit to really and truly enter into the paths of purity and simplicity in such a way that I merit to really perfect belief and to fulfill all Your Torah with love, truth, purity and simplicity all the days of my life.

"Let my heart be pure in Your statutes so that I will not be ashamed". For "You are the Lord, God, who chose Abram and brought him out of Ur of the Chaldees and gave him the name Abraham. And found his heart to be faithful before You". He walked before You in purity and simplicity, for he was the first of all the true, pure and honest believers who serve You in purity and simplicity, in truth and perfect belief. In his merit and the merit of all the true, pure tzaddikim, have mercy upon me and let me merit to begin now to go in Your ways, with purity and simplicity, with truth and perfect belief. Remove from my heart its stubbornness so that I will not lead my heart into foolishness, into paths of worthless wisdoms that are so customary in the world, wisdoms that severely confuse and prevent us from thinking about our purpose in life, our final end and how to really come closer to You. Let me clear out and drive out from my heart all these wisdoms. May I really and truly know the immensity of my foolishness and how much I lack perception, as is written, "Surely I am more brutish than any man and haven't the understanding of a man". And it is written: "I was brutish and without

Prayers from the Heart / Prayer 123

knowledge: I was like a beast before You". And, "I said I will be wise; but it was far from me". Have mercy upon me so that I will not mislead myself with any worldly wisdom which can confuse so much. Rather, may I merit to fulfill, with truth and purity, all that our true Sages say. Let me nullify my perception and intellect completely before them, as if I have no intellect at all, which is really the truth. May I merit to fulfill the verse which says: "Lord, who will abide in Your Tabernacle and who will dwell on Your holy Mount? He who walks in purity (simplicity), performs righteousness and speaks the truth in his heart".

May it be pleasing before You, Lord, our God and God of our Fathers, full of loving-kindness, who does much good, that, in Your bountiful compassion, You have mercy upon me. Show me, teach me and guide me in the ways of the real purity and simplicity, with perfect faith, without any worthless wisdoms at all. You know that we have no way to come close to You other than by complete purity and simplicity, with truth and perfect faith. I believe and understand from afar, that even in the depths of our descent at present, in the midst of the force of this bitter exile, in body and spirit, there are ways of purity and simplicity and faith. Every person, wherever he is (in terms of his spiritual level), can remove himself from his exile and descent by means of the pathways of purity and simplicity; he can find the straight way and correct advice, he can find You in every place, even he who has fallen to wherever he is fallen. Everyone can rise out of their fall and descent and can come close and attach themselves to You. They can please and appease You with purity and simplicity, with prayer, supplications, truth and perfect faith, for these You desire, as it says, "My eyes will be upon the faithful of the land that they may dwell with me. He who walks in a pure (simple) way, he will serve me". And it says: "Blessed are those whose path is simplicity, who walk in the Torah of the Lord". Let me merit to all that I have requested before You. May the words of my mouth and the meditation of my heart be pleasing before Your Countenance, O Lord, my Rock and Redeemer.

Prayer 125 – 126

Master of the World, let us merit to welcome properly the holiness of Shabbat. May I merit to fulfill the commandment of eating three meals every single Shabbat and to fulfill properly the commandment of delight on Shabbat, to eat, drink and have plenty of delights for the sake of Shabbat. You know how great is the virtue and the preciousness of eating on Shabbat. Grant us the merit to fulfill perfectly that which is written about eating on Shabbat: "…eat it today for today is a Shabbat for the Lord; today you will not find it in the field." From this the Sages learnt that a person must eat three meals on Shabbat for "today" is written three times. Let me merit to eat the Shabbat meals with great holiness and may I have in mind at every meal that now I am not eating for the delight (pleasure) of the body, nor as I eat during the weekdays, when it is the usual custom of people to eat not for the sake of a commandment but, rather, to stave off hunger; for these are meals we are permitted (but not commanded) to eat. Sometimes one eats because one is hungry from the day before and sometimes one eats so as not to be hungry the following day, but on Shabbat let me have in mind at every meal that I am eating only for the sake of the honour of the day, for the honour of Shabbat, which is an aspect of "eat it today, for today is a Shabbat of the Lord". Through this, may the days of the week have no hold or control over the holiness of eating on Shabbat, for then I eat only for the sake of Shabbat to fulfill the commandment of eating a Shabbat meal and not because I want to prevent being hungry on weekdays. May I have many good foods and drinks for the honour of Shabbat and may I know and believe with complete faith that eating on Shabbat is something else entirely from eating during the weekdays. Outside forces (outside the realm of holiness) have no hold whatsoever over our eating on Shabbat, for eating on Shabbat is all divine, all holy, as You informed us by Your holy Sages, may their memories be blessed. May I merit to draw holiness from the holiness of eating on Shabbat to my eating during the weekdays, as the Rabbis said of the sage Shamai, who used to eat for the sake of Shabbat every day, all throughout his entire life. May I also grasp the attribute of the sage Hillel, who used to say, "Blessed is the Lord every day".

Let me not think or worry from one day to another at all and let me merit to really feel in my heart the pleasantness (sweetness and delight) of the holiness of Shabbat, and to feel the holiness of the extra soul that comes to a person every Shabbat. May I welcome the extra soul of Shabbat immediately upon the entry of Shabbat and to feel in my heart the pleasantness of its holiness such that I immediately begin to long for and feel sorrow about the loss of the extra soul (after the end of Shabbat). May I merit by this to connect myself so much to the holiness of Shabbat and the holiness of the extra soul which comes on Shabbat that, during the weekdays also, there will remain with me a great impression of its holiness. Through this, may I also serve You sincerely during the weekdays and draw upon myself every time the holiness of Shabbat, and may I long for and desire very much to welcome the holiness of Shabbat, which comes with extra radiance and extra holiness, until I merit by this to really welcome every single Shabbat with extra holiness and the most tremendous radiance. May I welcome the extra soul, spirit and higher soul every single Shabbat in the greatest possible spiritual level and may I merit to come close to real tzaddikim who are themselves the aspect of Shabbat, as the Sages said. May I feel the pleasantness of their holiness, until, at all times (for many days and years), I will have in mind great sorrow and great longing because of my separation from them after they pass away, just like the group of students of Rabbi Shimon bar Yochai used to say when bemoaning the time when he would pass away. Let me merit to think about this and to attach myself so much to the pleasantness of their holiness during their lifetime that, through this I receive from them every time a great and true radiance in my mind, in my heart, in my soul, spirit and higher soul, even after they pass away; for tzaddikim after their death are called "alive". Even more so, tzaddikim are greater after their death than when they were alive!

Let me merit to hear Torah from the mouth of true tzaddikim and let me really feel the greatness of the wonder and awe of their new Torah insights such that I cannot stop myself from praising them in their presence. Through this, may I merit to have revealed to me more wonderful and awesome new Torah insights. So too also with the holiness of Shabbat. May I say many praises and sings songs of praise of Shabbat with great happiness, with wonderful and great yearning, such, that by this I merit to receive, even more so every time, the pleasantness of the holiness of Shabbat. Fulfill in me the verse which says: "If you turn away your foot from (violating) Shabbat" etc. "and call the Shabbat a delight, the holy of the Lord and honoured……. Then you shall delight yourself in the Lord and I will cause you to ride upon the high places of the earth and feed you with the heritage of Jacob your father: for the mouth of the Lord has spoken".

Prayer 127-128

Master of the Universe merit me to always wear new clothing that are complete and untorn for You have taught us that clothes are the secret of 'chashmal' a protective barrier. However, when clothes are torn this spoils the protection. Merit us to guard our clothes and to honour them properly, keeping them clean.

Please protect me so that I will not look at anything that can damage my eyes even if it is only a moment's glance out of the side of the eye. Merit me to fulfill the verses: "Do not follow after your heart and after you eyes" and "I have mad a covenant with my eyes".

Prayer 129

May it be Your will, O Lord, our God and God of our fathers, God of Faith, that You grant us merit, through Your bountiful mercy and immense loving kindness, to really perfect, wholehearted faith. May I merit to believe in You and in Your true tzaddikim with really perfect faith. May I merit to enter into, cleave to and be enveloped within perfect, holy faith. Let me be strong and bold in holy faith such that I merit to turn the materiality of my body into the essence of holy faith. May the holy faith consume me until all the evil which has a hold in me be devoured and nullified. Let me merit to turn from evil to good by way of perfect faith, so that I merit to be included and nullified totally within holy faith. Let me merit very speedily to come to the land of Israel with out harm and there to come close and cleave to true tzaddikim, with great attachment and really perfect belief.

In Your great compassion, have mercy upon me; do not repay me according to my sins. In Your mercy, open for me the gates of holy belief; help me enter into faith

Prayers from the Heart / Prayer 129

with truth, to be enveloped within it completely such that I merit to be consumed by faith and to turn into its holy essence, the essence of the holy Land of Israel, the essence of the holiness of true tzaddikim. Do not let the Land or the holy faith vomit me out as it did to the other nations who came before me. Even though I am not fitting or worthy to touch holy faith or the holy Land of Israel or to come close to real tzaddikim, for I have committed many evil deeds and spoilt my holiness, nevertheless, Lord, Your compassion is great. So have mercy upon me, help me, save me and grant me merit so that the holy faith will be able to stomach me within itself and to always retain me, until I become consumed and really changed into the essence of holy faith.

You, who are full of compassion, let me merit to perfect faith in all aspects, for we have no hope or support nowadays other than by holy faith. You know the immense yoke and force of the exile upon our souls because of the cravings of the body which overcome us all the time. Because of our many iniquities, we no longer have the strength to stand against them and break them and nullify them completely. We have only the strength of holy belief, that You will bring us into faith, such that we merit to be consumed by faith and change to the essence of holy faith. Our eyes, O Lord turn towards faith. In Your plentiful mercy, let me merit to really perfect, holy belief, as is Your desire. "All Your commandments are faith". "I will sing of the loving-kindness of the Lord forever; with my mouth I will make known Your faith to all generations". "For I have said: A world of loving-kindness will be built up: Your faith You will establish in the very heavens"... "Your faith is round about You". Fulfill in us the verse which says: "I will betroth you to Me in righteousness and in judgment and in loving-kindness and in mercies. I will betroth you to Me in faith and you will know the Lord". Blessed be the Lord forever. Amen and amen.

Prayer 130

I have stretched out my hands to You. Instruct and teach me Your paths of truth and Your upright advice at all times in such a way that I merit to quickly repent for having bad deeds and indecent thoughts. Then merit me, as a result, for a speedy rectification of the brit in a really complete way as You desire. Grant me true knowledge and intelligence so that I will know to truly feel my lowliness. Let no thought of pride or haughtiness come into my mind for according to my true worthlessness I should not have to pray at all to be saved from pride. Who am I that I should feel any pride!

But You know how strange thoughts of pride confuse my mind especially when I want to perform something in the realm of holiness.

Therefore I have come before You, Mercirful One, Who knows the hidden things, have compassion on me constantly and be with me on all occasions. Guard me always so that no thoughts of pride or haughtiness come into my heart at all. Rather, merit me to true humility in such a way that I achieve real holiness of the brit. You have already informed us throught Your holy sages that by humility one merits to guard the brit. But save us from false humility. Give me only genuine humility as You desire. May the words of my mouth and the meditations of my heart find favour before You, God, my Rock and Redeemer.

Prayer 133

I have come before You, God my God and God of our fathers, to ask that You have compassion upon me. Grant me advice, strength and encouragement how to block and remove my materialistic eyes and thoughts from looking at the vanities of this world from now on, especially when I begin to think about something which leads to indecent thoughts, Heaven forbid. For the truth

Prayers from the Heart / Prayer 133

is that I believe that we always have free choice. However because of the immense bitterness of my habits it is hard for me to hold my thoughts in the realm of holiness. But You can help me, for Your Name's sake, for the sake of Your honour, so save me from now on from whatever I have to be saved from.

Arouse Your mercy upon me and come to my assistance so that I merit to remove my eyes from looking at This World both materially and spiritually. Just let me turn my eyes, heart and mind to always look at the light of the Torah and the true Tzaddikim who shine with their great, awesome and sublime light. And may this nullify from me all the physical cravings of the world. I believe truthfully with complete faith that all This World and all its cravings and vanities are no more than a spec in comparison to the Torah and the Holy tzaddikim who shine throughout all the worlds with a great wonderful and awesome light. It is just that this world, which is so small in size and essence and quality, appears in front of the eyes of people and prevents or delays them from perceiving the great precious light of the Torah and the tzaddikim. Have mercy on us for Your Name's Sake. Let me not follow after my eyes; rather help me not to raise my eyes to look at the dealings of This World, its vanities and evil cravings which, in the end, are very bitter.

Direct my vision and sight towards the light of the Torah and the true tzaddikim at all times. By this, let all the cravings and affairs of This World be nullified from me. Merit me to spend all my days striving to come close to genuine tzaddikim and for the holy Torah which they draw down, reveal and radiate throughout the entire world all the time.

Help us for Your Name's Sake. Our Father and King, reveal the glory of Your Kingdom over us speedily through Your holy Torah and merit me from now on to repent fully and purely as You desire. Shine Your Countenance upon Your servant. Save us in Your loving kindness. Amen.

Prayer 135

May I find favour before You, O Lord, our God and God of our fathers, so that in Your bountiful mercy, I merit to really come close and attach myself to true tzaddikim, with real desire in my heart and soul, with really great, powerful love. Let me love them with such a great love that my love of them will be greater and more wonderful than the love for women, until all my love for women and craving for sex be nullified from me by my overwhelming love of the tzaddikim. Take pity and have mercy upon me; let me merit to real love of the tzaddikim and by this may I merit to attach myself very greatly and firmly to them. Let my soul be tied up in theirs in a very, very strong bond from now, forever until eternity, for eternities.

May it be Your will O Lord, our God and God of our fathers, that in Your bountiful mercy and tremendous loving-kindness, I merit to welcome all the Festivals and Holy Days with great holiness and purity, with great happiness and joy and wisdom, with absolute perfection as is really Your desire. May I behold the face of my rabbi on the Festival even when I am far from Him. (When you celebrate the Festivals fittingly it is equivalent to seeing your rabbi... This is true even if you and he are physically miles apart! – Torah 135 Likutei Moharan).

May I merit to behold the faces of the true tzaddikim, to recognize them and love them and to draw upon myself their holiness by welcoming the Holy festivals which are drawn from them. Through this, may I merit to the Forty-Nine Gates of Wisdom which are revealed and radiate on the Festivals. Open for me the light of the holy mind; let me merit to a great and wonderful power to really look into Your Torah and service. By this, may all the foolishness of all sorts of self-importance, pride and haughtiness be nullified. May I merit to completely perfect humility as is Your good desire. Always draw upon me and all of Israel the holiness of Moses, our teacher, may he rest in peace, who merited to real humility; as is written: "Now the man Moshe was very humble, more so than all other men on the face of the earth". Have mercy upon us, You who are full of compassion, that we merit, through the strength of welcoming the Festivals – "Festivals of the Lord, holy convocations" – to draw upon ourselves the holiness of all true tzaddikim. May all the true holy brains and intellect, drawn from the Festivals, be drawn upon us by them so that, by this, we merit to nullify and cast off from ourselves all sorts of self-importance, pride and extraneous motives. Through this, may we merit to real humility, to the humility of Moses, our teacher, may he rest in peace.

Master of the World, You know my great distance from true humility. "Surely I am more ignorant than any man and have not the understanding of a man". In my many iniquities I do not know at all what true humility is, for humility is greater than everything. Lord of compassion, have mercy upon me and let me merit to the real holiness of each Festival until I merit by this to know and acknowledge very well the virtue and the greatness of the true tzaddikim, until I nullify myself to them in utter self-nullification. By this, may all sorts of pride, haughtiness, self-importance and extraneous motives and everything else bad that one can talk of or think of be nullified automatically from me; such that I merit to real humility as is Your real desire.

Master of the World, let me merit to fear Your Name really and truly and wholeheartedly. Fulfill in us the verse which says "Through humility (comes) fear of God". Let me to merit return in complete repentance before You through the radiance of the holiness of the Festivals, for You have already revealed to us that the Festivals are days of judgment, days of repentance. Through this, may I merit to rectify all the blemishes that I caused to the aspect of the Kingdom of Holiness by my immense iniquities and willful transgressions. I caused, so to speak, the Kingdom of Holiness to fall. By this the four kingdoms of the Other Side became stronger, especially the husk of Amalek, may his name be wiped out, for he is the generality of all husks; as it says: "The first of the nations is Amalek". Therefore take pity and have mercy upon me and return me in complete repentance before You. Through this, may I merit to raise the holy Kingdom from its fall; so that all the four kingdoms of the Other Side be nullified, especially the kingdom of Amalek, may his name and memory be wiped out.

May I merit to come close to and really attach myself to true tzaddikim who occupy themselves with elevating the aspect of Kingdom. They create the principal holiness of the Festivals, which is the raising of the aspect of the

Kingdom of Holiness from among the husks and the nullifying of all the power and rule of the four kingdoms of the Other Side. Therefore, by attaching myself to true tzaddikim, maybe someone very lowly, rotten and insignificant as myself can also welcome the holiness of the Festivals such that I merit to real humility, true, holy fear and to perfect repentance and speedy redemption; as the rabbis of bless memory said: Repentance is great since it brings closer the redemption".

Prayer 136

My Father in Heaven. Assist me and save me so that I may judge every Jew on the side of merit, even those who incite controversy against true tzaddikim and even insult them. Merit me to fulfill that which the Sages said. "Do not judge your fellow until you arrive at his place". In this way may all the controversy in the world be nullified and let great peace be drawn down so that all Jews become united.

In Your bountiful mercy, help me to repent quickly with a complete repentance before You, in truth until I reach the holiness and virtue of all those Jews who are above me in their holiness and purity; that I truly reach their place and unite with them with truth and great peace. And, if

Prayers from the Heart / Prayer 136

on the contrary, their dispute against us is because they are far and lower than us and therefore, they are jealous and argue against us, then, please have mercy on us for Your name's sake and merit us to judge them favourably at all times and teach us, in your abundant mercy, to find in them merits and goodness even in the fact that they dispute with us. In such a way may I raise them up and cause them to enter them into the scales of merit. Then they will unite with us totally and perfectly and controversy will be nullified from among all the Jewish people. Please put into the hearts of those who oppose and dispute the truth the thought that they retract all their hate and controversy and instead pursue truth and peace. And those who hate and oppose the truth, who do not really desire peace, subdue them and bring them down to the dust.

Have mercy for Your Name's sake. Place peace in the world for You know how much controversy damages the Jewish People. Merciful One, in Your awesome wonders, act to draw down real peace into the world. Fulfill the verse: "May He who makes peace in the Heavens, bring peace upon us and upon all the Jewish People. Amen.

Prayer 137-138

Master of the Universe, help me to nullify and subdue the coarseness of my body; it opposes the light of my neshama which is a holy portion from Above. Merit me to hear well in my heart what my neshama tells me and teaches me about keeping Your commandments. Purify my heart to serve You truthfully. May I subdue and nullify the evil urge that dwells in my heart until 'my heart is a void within me'. Help me to purify and cleanse my heart from all kinds of extraneous and bad thoughts. Merit me to be totally honest with a pure heart. Through this, may the truth of the light of Godliness be revealed and shine in my heart, for you informed us that the heart of each Jew is full of Godliness.

Purify my heart so much that I will be able to know future events for my heart talks to me. Merit me that everything my heart tells me will really be the word of God.

Prayer 140

Please merit me to come close to true tzaddikim and to really believe in them. Even though I have no real grasp of them and their great holiness, nevertheless, help me to have a little understanding of the great virtue of the tzaddikim by seeing the excellence of those who are attached to them and serve You with perfect fear. Therefore, merit me not to have any doubts or questions about the true tzaddikim. Rather may I really believe in them even though I have no grasp of their spiritual level, for they are far beyond our human intelligence. Merit me to be counted among their followers and to come close to true tzaddikim. Let me listen to their advice and perform everything they teach me so that, by this, I can reach complete success, spiritually and materially in This World and the World to Come. Amen, may it be so.

Prayer 141

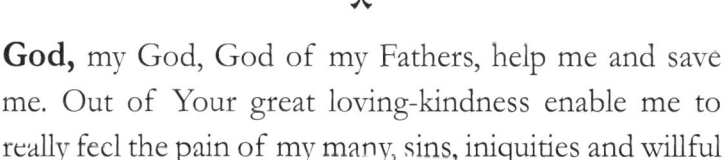

God, my God, God of my Fathers, help me and save me. Out of Your great loving-kindness enable me to really feel the pain of my many, sins, iniquities and willful sins which are vast, reaching as they do to the heights of the heavens. This is especially true regarding blemishes of the brit. I have spoiled the drops of the brain by expending them wastefully, whether intentionally or not. If I were to begin to feel the pain of the immensity of this great and awesome sin, I do not know if I could survive even an hour. You informed us, through Your true tzaddikim the seriousness of this blemish. It causes the extension of the destruction of the holy Temple, delays the Redemption and causes the Shechinah to descend into exile, Heaven forbid. We draw enslaved souls into the realm of the husks and from each wasted sperm we create damaging forces, Heaven preserve us. Through this we spoil all the twenty-two letters of the Torah which are included in the drops of semen.

The truth is that my heart is so blocked, confused and crooked that I do not feel the pain of my sins at all, despite their immensity. And even if I say 'oih and woe' a thousand times I still do not feel the pain at all.

Help me to speedily merit to return to You in repentance with all my heart. Open my heart in such a way that I will really feel the pain of my enormous sins. Just let me shout out from my heart, a great and bitter scream as is fitting to shout out about my sins. I will shout out to You with all my heart, with a truly broken heart until all the hearts of all the wasted sperm will feel it, wherever they got drawn to. Then all their hearts will be circumcised such that they feel the immense pain and distress of

Prayers from the Heart / Prayer 142

their being in the depths of hell and places of filth. Let me make such a great noise among these drops that they are all aroused to return to You. May they start to feel remorse and really long for a rectification.

Please God, deal with our rectification and redeem us speedily from all the filthy and spoilt places. Circumcise our hearts so we will love Your Name. Merit me very soon to circumcise the foreskin of my heart and the hearts of my offspring, especially during the holy days of Elul. Help me to prepare myself so that in the month of Elul I will merit to fully circumcise my heart and those of my children As a result, may the true tzaddikim rectify me and my family completely during my lifetime.

Prayer 142

"**My** soul desired and even longed for the courts of God; my heart and my flesh sing out for the living God".

"**My** soul thirsts for You; my flesh longs for You in a dry and thirsty land where there is no water."

"**My** soul thirsts for God, for the living God; when will I come and appear before God."

Master of the World, You know how very great the obstacles are that I now face in all the things related to holiness such as Torah, prayer and good deeds. It is impossible to clarify even the minutest part of the many confusions and obstacles and delays that I encounter in everything to do with holiness. Even when I perform some commandment, or do something holy, it is very, very confused and muddled. It is very far away from the perfection of the rectification that we need to accomplish by each commandment, for, through my many iniquities, I have become very distant from Your Torah and Your commandments. In my own eyes I am really like someone wandering, lost in the desert, in a place of darkness and bleakness, of very great darkness. I do not have any idea at all what to do so as to return to the true, straight and proper path, to be really, perfect as You desire. I walk in the ephemeral world. "I am like a drunken man and like someone overcome with wine" wandering to and fro. I am confused and mixed up with thousands and tens of thousands of confusions upon confusions and multiple obstacles which prevent me and confuse me from truly perfectly coming closer to You and Your Torah — for which purpose I was created. What will I do on the day of reckoning? "What shall I do when God rises up? When He visits judgment, what shall I answer Him?" I do not know at all with what to revive my very, very miserable and bitter soul, which is blemished and mixed up so very much, other than

Prayers from the Heart / Prayer 142

longing, yearning and wanting to come closer to You, to Your service and to Your Torah, for there is an immense virtue to holy desire and longing, as revealed to us by our holy Sages.

Therefore, I have come before You, my Father in Heaven, my Father, Father of mercy, who grants good even to the guilty. Grant me much good and let me merit to always yearn for, long for and desire You, Your service and Your Torah with intense longing and strong and forceful desire; until, in Your mercy, I merit to learn a great deal every day and to recite many prayers, supplications, requests, tunes and songs of praise, every single day. Help me to perform many commandments and good deeds every single day of my life. Even when, according to Your desire, there is a need to stop learning etc. and even if sometimes I am in places where it is impossible to learn and to engage in Your service, grant me merit and help me that I have a craving and strong desire to learn Torah and to really serve You until this desire rises before You and is considered as if I actually performed a commandment or learnt Torah. You, who are full of compassion, have mercy upon me and help me to start training myself to always yearn for, long for and desire Your Torah and Your service very strongly and sincerely, and to really come closer to You. Through this real desire and willpower in the heart, may I merit to

Prayers from the Heart / Prayer 142

learn from the Supernal Book, written on the Supernal Heart by the true tzaddikim, for You hearken and listen to the words of each one of them in his own place.

You join them together and write from them a book of remembrance for those who think in their heart and really desire to learn Your Torah and to do Your will, as is written: "Then they who feared the Lord and thought about His Name". Let me merit also to receive and draw upon myself a great radiance from this Supernal Heart and to learn from this Supernal Book. I am far away from everything but I anticipate Your mercy and Your loving-kindness and that You will grant me the merit to a real desire and longing to come closer to You, to Your service and to Your Torah. Let it be in such a way that I quickly, sincerely return to You, as is Your good desire. Take pity and have mercy upon me in Your bountiful mercy, in Your great mercy. Help me, for I have relied upon You for support. "For You are the glory of their strength; in Your favour our horn will be exalted". " May the words of my mouth and the meditation of my heart be pleasing before Your Countenance, O God, my Rock and my Redeemer". Amen and Amen.

Prayer 143

"**You** will guide me with Your advice and afterwards receive me to glory". Master of the World, my King, my God, to You I will pray…Have mercy upon me for Your Name's sake, for You know how great is the lack of advice and how immense are the doubts I have about everything. Usually my advice is ambiguous. I do not know how to give counsel to my soul about anything, whether important or insignificant. This greatly prevents me from serving God and from true repentance. Master of Compassion, have mercy upon me. "Great in advice and mighty in deed", let me merit to always accept all the advice from the true tzaddikim and really righteous people of the generation whose advice all comes from the Torah and they received it from their rabbis, the holy, true tzaddikim. May we merit to really come close to them and to accept their advice about everything in the world, whether worship of God, trading, business, money matters and all other things. Let me ask their advice with regard to all things and let me merit to receive counsel and wisdom from them. Let their wisdom radiate within me and by this, let great loving-kindness be drawn upon me. Sweeten and nullify from upon me all the harsh judgments in the world. Let me merit to complete salvation at all times, as it says: "There is salvation in the multitude of counsel". Protect me and save me at all times so that I never stumble because of bad advice, Heaven forbid. Save me from drawing upon myself any anguish, suffering or damage. Heaven forbid, by foolish advice, Heaven forbid. Rather, let me always strive to accept all advice from the real tzaddikim and righteous people of the generation, in such a way that their holy wisdom radiate within me. Arouse Your great mercy and loving-kindness upon me at all times; always save me from what I need to be saved from, both physically and spiritually…May the words of my mouth and the contemplation of my heart find favour before You, O Lord, my Rock and my Redeemer. Blessed be the Lord forever. Amen and Amen.

Prayer 144 – 145

You who revive the dead with great compassion; in Your bountiful mercy, revive me and preserve me and save me so that I merit from now on to conquer my evil urge and help me to always be in complete control of my desires, even the desires that are permitted, even on the day when food and drink are permitted. With regard to these desires, let me merit to behave, in great holiness and

Prayers from the Heart / Prayer 144 – 145

purity for Your Name's sake alone, without any desire of the body at all. Master of the World, say to my troubles, 'Enough!' Quickly deliver me a complete salvation from all the desires of This World. Take pity and have mercy upon my wretched soul, which has already been blemished a great deal by evil desires, as You know. In Your great compassion and great loving-kindness, have pity upon me, from now on, and grant me the power and might and true advice at all times in such a way that I merit to nullify all my desires completely, until I merit to the true life, the eternal life, in This World and in the World to Come. Even when the time comes for me to depart from the world let there be no difference for me between life and after death. Rather, let it all be the same. Let me always merit to serve You truly, whether whilst alive in This World or whether after my passing on to the World to Come, such that I always be alive even after my passing away. Let me live and never die. Let me be amongst the tzaddikim who, even after their death, are called 'alive'. "I will walk before the Lord in the land of the living". I shall not die but shall live and recount the deeds of God".

Master of the World, save me from dispute. Help me and save me so that I can hold back my desire for discord. Let me not have any desire to be involved in dispute, Heaven forbid, rather let me always try with all my might to quieten the dissension and dispute. May I always really chase after peace until, by this I merit to have people learning as a Torah law my innovations in Torah, in my name after my departure from This World. May my lips murmur in the grave and let me merit to live in two worlds and never die. Rather, let me always be really within the generality of life.

Prayer 146

Master of the Universe, You informed us that even when the physical cravings of a person are at their strongest such that it is difficult to break them or hold himself back from them, even so the Torah stands by a person and calls him, announcing: 'Until when, fools, will you love folly'? And even though he may not hear the call because of his cravings, after the craving finishes he will immediately hear the call. As a result he will feel regret about the sin or craving; for he heard the wisdom of the Torah which makes the fool wise. You also revealed to us how the Torah gives witness about man's deeds, since it stands after a person and calls him even at the time when he acts indiscreetly. Therefore, have mercy on us so that we remember each time that the Torah is united with You. As a result, it goes with us

Prayers from the Heart / Prayer 147

to all the lowliest and dirtiest places and calls us to turn aside from the paths of hell and death.

Through this we can break all our cravings and because of the immense shame and fear of God, we will have fear of the holy Torah which stands before us and constantly calls to us. How can we raise our heads before You when the Torah itself gives witness about our deeds?

Master of the Universe, have mercy on us from now on and merit us to abandon our evil ways very speedily. Let us return to You, for You are bountiful in Your forgiveness.

Prayer 147

Merit me to holy audacity so that I can be as bold as a leopard. Let me have holy audacity against all those who stand in my way preventing me from serving God, Heaven Forbid. Help me to be very strong in my boldness against them. Let me never be ashamed at all by their mockery nor spend time arguing with them. On the contrary, however much they rise against me to stop me from Torah and Prayer , may my holy boldness just become that much stronger, so that I can break all the obstacles. Someone who lacks this holy boldness lacks a portion in the holy Torah for the main strength in Torah and serving God depends on this holy boldness. This boldness adds strength and might in the World Above, so to speak. Then, from Above, they in turn add strength and holy boldness to the person so he can withstand all the obstacles and break them. Please help me to begin and also to bring to completion anything I want to achieve in the service of God.

Similarly, merit me to find the right path in the attribute of humility so that I can be very lowly and humble in relation to all other people. However, let me not be lowly and worthless in my own eyes such that I feel ashamed when mockers stand in the way of my serving God. On the contrary may I strengthen myself with holy boldness against them. Let me not take any notice of them at all. Then draw upon me a radiance of the true humility of Moses.

Prayer 148

Merit me to perfect fear of God, as it says: "The heel of humility is fear of God". "The beginning of wisdom is fear of God". There exists one fear above another. Let me go from one level of fear to progressively higher levels. Merit me to draw upon myself, Your holy fear from a successively higher level such that I achieve loftier and loftier levels in the attribute of fear, without end. Amen, so may it be.

Prayer 149

"**At** midnight I will rise to give thanks to You because of Your righteous judgments". You, who are full of mercy, who awakens the sleepers and arouses the slumberers. Take pity and have compassion upon me; in Your bountiful mercy, let me merit to rise every single night of my life at exactly midnight. Let me merit to awaken from my sleep at exactly midnight, with tremendous speed and without any laziness or difficulty at all. Do not let sleep or slumber overcome me, Heaven forbid.

Do not let anything prevent me from this.

In Your bountiful mercy and great loving-kindness awaken the northern wind which blows through the harp of King David at midnight, and from there let there be drawn upon me a spiritual arousal, so that I always awaken from my sleep at midnight. 'Awaken, my honorable soul awaken; with the lyre and harp I will awaken the dawn".

Master of the World. You warned us in several ways to always rise at midnight, as is written in the holy Zohar where there are awesome warnings about this.

Prayers from the Heart / Prayer 149

However, You know that the obstacles have multiplied and overcome each one of us, preventing us from this, such that most nights we have not managed to rise at midnight. Therefore, Master of all, abundantly strong to save, I have come before You; give me advice how to merit to this, to always rise at exactly midnight which is immediately after six hours from the beginning of the night, both in summer and winter. Let me awaken then with great speed and say the Midnight Prayer; to mourn and wail over the destruction of the Holy Temple; over the exile of the Torah whose secrets have been passed to external forces; and over my many and enormous sins, iniquities and willful transgressions which have caused all this and lengthened the exile so much. Maker of all, it is clear to You how very much I have lengthened the exile because of my many transgressions, both generally and specifically. Oh, Oh, woe is me! What can I say? What can I speak? How can I justify myself? Behold, I stand before You in great guilt. What has passed has passed. Let me merit from now on to truly return to the straight path. Let me not lose any night of my nights by not rising at midnight. Always be with me; help me and guard me so that rising at midnight will not harm me in any way at all. Let me not suffer any headache or any harm from this. My Father in Heaven, raise me and hasten me. Grant me merit from now on always to rise

Prayers from the Heart / Prayer 149

exactly at midnight, every night whether on a weekday, Shabbat or Festival, whether at home or traveling and to recite the midnight prayer to sweeten and nullify all the harsh judgments from upon myself and all my family and all Your Nation, the sons of Israel.

Let me look at the heavens every morning and by this, help me to draw upon myself holy perception, a refined and pure perception, a true perception by which I can merit to really return to You, to be really as You desire from now on and forever. Let there be drawn upon me every morning a thread of loving-kindness from the 'morning of Abraham". May you fulfill the verse which states: "The Lord will command His loving-kindness in the daytime and in the night His song shall be with me; a prayer to the God of my life (who gives life)". And it says, "Your loving-kindness O Lord is in the heavens; Your faithfulness reaches to the clouds". And it says, "They are new every morning; great is Your faithfulness". May the words of my mouth and the meditation of my heart be pleasing before Your Countenance, O God, my Rock and my Redeemer. Amen and Amen.

Prayer 151

"**New** moons You gave to your People as a time of atonement for all their offspring" Master of the Universe, merit me, among all the Jewish People to bring up my children to Torah, marriage and good deeds. Save us, from now on, from all kinds of anguish regarding our children. Draw upon us and our offspring long life. Master of the World, You informed us that the death of small children, Heaven preserve us, stems from the blemishing (waning) of the moon for this indicates a lack of light which leads to children's illnesses, Heaven forbid. But on Rosh Chodesh (the first day of the new month) the moon's light begins to grow and become rectified. This is the time of atonement for all our offspring. Then, atonement, forgiveness and a sweetening of harsh decrees are drawn into the world. Therefore please merit us, in Your great mercy, to receive the holiness of the first day of each month, as is fitting. May it be Your will that You raise us in joy and return us to our land and there, we will bring sacrifices before You both the obligatory continual offerings and the additional offerings of Rosh Chodesh. Let us bring them before You with love, as we are commanded.

Prayers from the Heart / Prayer 152

You know that when we learn or recite the passages about sacrifices it is considered by You as if we had actually brought them at their proper time and place. Therefore, may it be Your will that by reciting the passage "on the first day of each month" whenever we do, even when not on a Rosh Chodesh, it should be considered as if we had brought the sacrifice on Rosh Chodesh itself. By this, draw down a rectification and fullness to the moon. And by this, bestow upon us atonement, forgiveness and a sweetening of harsh decrees. And may all the offspring of the Jewish People merit to have good long lives. Enable us to perform the commandment of blessing the new moon every month in the proper time, as You desire. Amen.

Prayer 152

Master of the Universe Who forgives and pardons our sins. As a free gift, grant us lovingly Your holy faith. Merit us to real belief in Torah scholars and tzaddikim. Save us so that we can enter the gateways of holiness and really come close to genuine tzaddikim. Have mercy on us in Your bountiful compassion and grant us complete faith, really and truly. You know we have no hope apart from faith in the tzaddikim; without them we cannot raise our hands or legs. Do it for Your Name's sake. Don't ever throw us away from holy belief. Don't close the entrance. Please don't lock the door in our face, Heaven forbid. Have compassion upon the Jewish People. How will someone like me, filthy with bad deeds, enter the gateway of holiness which is holy belief? How can I come close to the true tzaddikim who are the source of my soul?

Open up for me the entrances to the realm of holiness. Bestow upon me Your holy belief so that I will merit to be bold, strong and consistent in my holy belief, believing in true tzaddikim, coming close to them and drawing vitality from their holy wisdom. Break, uproot and nullify all the husks and forces of evil that encircle them. All the opposition to the tzadddikim, doubts, questions and confusions about them stem from these husks. So, please open for us the gateways of faith in such a way that no husk or evil force will have the strength to hide the truth from us or close the gateway, Heaven forbid. Master of the World, full of compassion have mercy on us and command all the guards that stand in the entranceway to be nullified and driven away. Remove the barriers from the entrance.

Help me and my offspring and all Jewish children to have real self-sacrifice being prepared to give away our bodies and souls and money in order to come close to

Prayers from the Heart / Prayer 153

the true tzaddik in such a way that we draw from his holy wisdom. God, please redeem us speedily both generally and individually. Don't caste us away from before You and don't take from us the spirit of Your holiness. Don't caste us into old age or desert us. When our strength fails, open the gateway for us before it is locked. Many days and years of our lives have already passed and the gateways of holiness are still closed to us; they are locked in our face because of our many iniquities and immense sins. Arouse Your mercy over such a poor soul as myself who has been standing near the entrance for many years. Don't hide Your countenance from me. May the words of my mouth and the meditations of my heart find favour before You, God, my Rock and Redeemer.

Prayer 153

Master of the Universe, please allow me to come close to true tzaddikim and Torah scholars. Merit me to receive their holy faces each time, such that I acquire a great radiance in my face from the light of their holy countenance, just as the moon reflects the light of the sun. Merit me to attach myself to the tzaddikim so much that I actually receive the light of their countenance in my face. May the countenance of the tzaddik or Torah

Prayers from the Heart / Prayer 153

scholar then be seen in my face. By this, merit me to a face of the tzaddik or Torah scholar; that they should be seen in my face. By this, merit me to a face of brightness and save me from all forms of darkness in the face which stems especially from the craving for money. When a person has a face of darkness (of worry and sadness) he cannot receive the holy countenance of the tzaddik in his own face. Furthermore, save me from arrogance, for someone who is arrogant has no face of holiness. Then he certainly cannot receive the light of the face of the tzaddik in his own face.

Merit me, each time, to talk to the true tzaddik and to hear Torah innovations from him, face to face. Then let me merge with him and become truly attached to him, becoming totally united with his holy words. Merit me to nullify myself to his holy words completely so that there is no separation between me and his holy words. May it be as if his holy words come from me. This is an aspect of "God spoke face to face with them", at Mount Sinai. As a a result, merit me to have all the tzaddik's holy words carved within my heart such that they shine and radiate into my soul, spirit and neshama, for ever and ever, for all eternity. Amen. So may it me.

Prayer 154

"**The** Lord, the Lord, God, merciful and gracious, long-suffering and abundant in goodness and truth". In Your bountiful mercy let me merit and all of Israel to have real desires, yearnings and longings to come to the Land of Israel, until I merit, in Your bountiful mercy and immense loving-kindness to manage to turn these desires into deeds, to travel and reach the Land of Israel, the holy Land, because of my very great distance from You and because of the immenseness of my materiality, the crookedness in my heart and the confusion of my mind. Because of all this I need to be in the Land in which the primary pillar of the source of holy belief exists. There, is found the root of the generality of the holiness of Israel. It is the Land which the Lord chose for His Chosen People, Israel. It is the Land which God always cares for, the Land of true life, eternal life; a desirable, good and spacious land which You gave to our fathers as an inheritance in favour, a land in which is found the "city of our God, the Mount of His Sanctuary. Fair in situation, the joy of all the land".

Please Lord, merciful One, full of compassion; charitable One, full of loving-kindness. Good One who is full of good, Tzaddik, full of righteousness. Savior,

Prayers from the Heart / Prayer 154

full of deliverance. Do good with me, as is Your desire. Let me merit, out of compassion and loving-kindness and as a gift, to come very quickly to the Land of Israel, the holy Land, the Land which our forefathers inherited, the land in which all the true tzaddikim really desired and longed to be. Most of them came there and rectified whatever they did and merited to whatever they merited , accomplishing everything through the holiness of the Land of Israel which is the focal point of holiness of the whole world. Abraham, the Patriarch, worked and strived very many years to get there. He beheld, saw, understood, searched, sealed, cut out, measured and counted until God revealed to him the holy Land, which is the foundation of the focal point of holiness, the foundation of belief; He promised him to give it as an inheritance to his offspring and their descendants in each of the generations. Therefore have mercy upon us for Your Name's sake. Even though I am completely and utterly despicable and worthless, in the merit and strength of Abraham and all the tzaddikim who merited to come to Israel, let me also merit quickly to skip and jump over all the obstacles, delays and disputes that prevent me from traveling to the Land of Israel. Let me break very quickly all the obstacles and come very speedily to the holy Land of Israel.

Prayers from the Heart / Prayer 154

Please, my Father, Merciful Father, have mercy upon me, a wretched, poor person as myself who pleads before You, who asks for charity, for an undeserved present. I have also not merited to tell the truth because of the greatness of the confusion and stupefaction of my mind, as is known to You, compassionate Lord. Even so, I await Your salvation, Your goodness, Your great loving-kindness, Your awesome and wonderful righteousness. Take pity and have mercy upon me. Bring me quickly and safely to the Land of Israel. Strengthen and embolden my mind and heart so that I merit to overcome all the obstacles, delays and confusions and all the obstacles of the mind. Grant me plenty of money for the expenses and everything needed on the trip. May I travel peacefully and arrive to the Land of Israel, safely in terms of my body, my Torah and my money. May I arrive safely without any harm. Save me from all sorts of bad thoughts and all sorts of blemishes. Let me not be hurt, Heaven forbid, by anything in the world during this long journey, whether in body, soul or monetarily, whether materially or spiritually.

May I leave in peace and arrive in peace. May I merit to achieve all my needs there, in the Land of Israel, and to really come closer to You by way of the holiness of the Land of Israel; may I rise spiritually from level to level in great holiness and purity, as is Your good desire

Prayers from the Heart / Prayer 154

May I merit, by the holiness of the Land of Israel, to break the attribute of anger completely. May I have patience in all its aspects, so that I always overcome my anger. Let me not be angry or strict about anything in the world. Rather, let me serve You perfectly and faithfully, with great simplicity and may I learn Torah and pray with tremendously great devotion and put all my strength and the thoughts of my heart and my mind into each and every word of the very, very holy and awesome prayers. May I know and believe with perfect faith that the whole world is full of Your glory.

You hear and listen to every word of prayer. Let me know before whom I stand, before the King of Kings, the Holy One. Through this may I draw upon myself great fear and awe of You. Help me to concentrate very well on every word without letting my mind wander from any word of prayer and its meaning. Save me from any extraneous thoughts during the time of prayer. Rather, merit me to attach my mind to the words of prayer very firmly indeed. As a result allow me to become stronger and stronger in Torah and prayer. Merit me to perform good deeds with great zeal and tremendous joy. I do not want to take any notice of any distraction or confusion, obstacle or delay. Help me not to be confused by them at all. Save me from any laziness, sadness or weakness of mind. On the contrary, in Your boundless mercy, help me through holy faith to break and completely nullify all kinds of laziness, heaviness and obstacles from the mind or from physical things. Let me nullify sadness, depression, improper thoughts, confusions and crookedness of the heart. Then merit me to the trait of real patience so that I can overcome and ignore all the obstacles and confusions. Let me not pay any attention to them at all. Bestow upon me the power to grow and flourish in Your service which stems from faith. Guard me so that nothing damages me at all. Anything that I do in the service of God, in Torah and mitzvoth, may I always be successful. For Your Name's sake do it.

Prayer 156

You, who are full of mercy, holy and awesome One, who purifies the impure, speedily purify my heart, pardon me with regard to the past; help me and save me in the future so that I merit to drive out and remove from my heart all the evil thoughts and all the confused ideas and all sorts of blemished thoughts that are in the heart. Let me extricate, drive out and remove them from my heart and may I strengthen myself and embolden myself at all times, so that I direct my heart towards You. Merciful One, Full of Compassion, let me merit

Prayers from the Heart / Prayer 156

to fervour, to holy enthusiasm of the heart. Act for the sake of our ancestors and sages and true tzaddikim, who bring righteousness to the public as stars that shine forever more. Grant me merit, in their strength, to also be amongst those who bring righteousness to the many. Let me judge each person on the side of merit and to bring many people closer to Your worship, to fear of You and to Your Torah. May I shine and radiate and inform all of Your People, Israel of Your truth; let my sincere words enter their hearts such that their hearts be warmed with great and holy enthusiasm and fervour to really return to You. By this, may increasingly great warmth and enthusiasm be drawn upon me every time. Let me merit to always receive and draw into my heart, holy enthusiasm and fervour from our rabbis, our teachers, the tazddikim who cleave to You, O Lord, our God. They receive fire from above, "burning coals of fire", in order to enflame and warm the hearts of Israel with holy enthusiasm and fervour thought their very words being like burning coals from the fire. Take pity on Your people Israel, so that their holy fire of enthusiasm never be extinguished. Fulfill in us the verse which says: "Let the fire on the altar be kept burning; let it not go out". May we all merit to receive their holy fire all the time, so as to warm and enthuse the heart of Your People, Israel, with holy fervour towards You, to serve

You truly in the right degree and measure, as is Your good desire. However much You give merit to instill holy enthusiasm and fervour in the hearts of others, so let me merit to have added and drawn upon me, many more times over, holy enthusiasm of the heart and fervour from Above, in the merit of our ancestors, teachers and tzaddikim who perform Your will, – "Your servants, a flaming fire". By this, may I extricate, drive out and remove from my heart all the spirit of foolishness and all the evil thoughts and ideas, such, that I soon merit to real purity of the heart. And through this, may I truly speak new, holy, pure words before You every time, to make You want to speedily bring me closer to You, so that I will always really cleave to You. May the words of my mouth and the meditation of my heart find favour before You, O Lord, my Rock and Redeemer.

Prayer 157

May it be Your will, O Lord, my God and God of my fathers, that You grant me the merit to cleave to Your holy Torah. Open my heart and my mind until I merit to hear and understand well, in my heart, all the words of Your holy, pure and perfect Torah which 'returns the soul and makes wise the fool; that gladdens the heart and enlightens the eyes, exists forever and is harmonious and righteous'. May I merit to feel very clearly the wonderful pleasure of the delight and sweetness of the new, holy and very awesome interpretations of the Torah which the true tzaddikim revealed and which give life to all the worlds. Let me enjoy and take delight in the Lord, in the words of Your holy Torah, such that I loathe and despise the life of This World, with its desires and vanities! May all the life of This World be nullified completely in my eyes, by the greatness of the pleasure, delight and enjoyment that I merit to get from the words of Your holy, awesome Torah, whose every word lives and exists, is faithful and delightful forever. "They are more desirable than gold, than much fine gold; sweeter than honey and the honeycomb".

For really, from a distance I see in my mind the pleasantness of the depth of Your Torah, whose every single word ascends to Ein Sof (the Infinite) and descends without end; whose each word ties, joins and includes all the worlds together; whose every word gives wonderful advice to all those whether on a high level or a low level, how to merit to know You and to really cleave to You. "How great are Your deeds O Lord, how infinitely profound Your thoughts". If we were to merit to listen and incline our ears and hearts very well to one word of Your holy Torah which You

Prayers from the Heart / Prayer 157

revealed to us by Your servant Moses and by all the true tzaddikim in every generation until today, we would become nullified completely! However, because of our many iniquities we do not merit to transfer the mind into the heart and through this to nullify the cravings of the heart. For our hearts are full of extraneous thoughts, cravings, confusions, reflections and crookedness, such that our hearts are very far away from the words of Your holy Torah. Therefore we do not feel the delight and sweetness of its pure words. Please, One and only Lord, who teaches Torah to His Nation, Israel, have mercy upon us for Your Name's sake. Open our hearts by our learning Your Torah. Let our hearts really cleave to the words of Your holy Torah, until we merit to enjoy and take great delight in the words of Your holy Torah, such that, through this, we despise all the life of This World, its desires and vanities. Grant us really good, long lives and let us cleave to You and to Your holy Torah and commandments forever. Let us not stray from Your desire, to the right or to the left. Please, O Lord, our God, cause the words of Your Torah to be a delight in our mouths so that we, and our descendants and the descendants of Your Nation, the House of Israel, may all know Your Name and learn Your Torah for its own sake, until we merit "to behold the beauty of the Lord and to visit His Temple", from now and forever. Amen, Selah.

Prayer 159

Master of the World, Who bestows the Torah, help me and save me; merit me to study Torah by day and by night. Sanctify us in Your commandments and give us a portion in Your Torah. Purify my thoughts and heart so that I can serve You without ulterior motives and study Torah for Your sake alone. All for God alone. Help me at all times to sanctify and purify myself properly so that all my studying will be for the sake of the Shechinah which is an intermediary between the world and the Holy One. May the Holy Shechinah accept all my Torah study with great love. Through this, draw upon us all sorts of bounty created by our studying, both spiritual and material bounty. Let the bounty from our studying Torah rise and give vitality to all the worlds above, all the angels, the Seraphim, Ophanim and holy Chayot. And may material bounty descend to all the Jewish People from our studies. Bestow upon us children, long life and a good livelihood in great plenty and holiness.

So also, have mercy upon us and help us so that all the vapours and air that we breathe in from the Torah

Prayers from the Heart / Prayer 159

of simple, lowly Jews who do not merit to raise their Torah to the Shechinah, be for the good. Merit us to turn these vapours, that are scattered through the air at night into the dew of Torah, heavenly lights and an elixir of life. As a result, merit us to arouse ourselves everyday with renewed desire and longing to engage ourselves in studying the Torah. May Your holy Torah be completely new in our eyes each day. Merit us to rise from one level to another in Your sublime holiness until I manage to create genuine Torah innovations from the vapours of other People, as You desire.

Guard and save us in Your immense compassion, so that these fallen vapours will not harm us, causing us to chase after business affairs with great efforts. Please, save us from the craving for money and all the burdens of this world and its vanities.

I cast all my hopes upon You and trust that You will bestow upon me a good livelihood so that I can put all my yearning into studying Torah and serving You, day and night. Then, may I feel renewed spiritual arousal, every day and every hour, with great desire to cleave to You, Your Torah and Your Service, with all my heart, from now on and forever. Amen, Selah.

Prayer 160

God, our God and God of our Fathers, may it find favour before You that I merit to always receive through the breath of my breathing, holy and pure vapours which stem from holy words and through this give me a holy pulse. In Your bountiful compassion, help me so that my pulse will always beat for the good and remind me through the pulse of the service of God blessed be He, as it is written "Listen! My beloved, knocks – let me in, my sister, my beloved, my dove, my flawless one. For my head is drenched with dew, my locks with the nighttime shower". Guard me and save me from the spirit of folly, from the evil spirit. Don't let me breathe any bad air or spirit which stems from the Other Side, caused from blemished words and protect me and guard me and save me from any pulse of the Other Side and may the pulse not have any power to remind me of the physical cravings and vanities of the This World, God Forbid. Through this protection, guard me and save me from any sin or iniquity from now on and forever. Please, Merciful One, in Your bountiful compassion do whatever is necessary in your great mercy and immense loving kindness in such a way that I merit to return to You quickly. Lord of wonders, The One who gives life to the living, Who remembers the forgotten, make my pulse beat for the good and remind me at all times to return to you, such that I merit to true and complete repentance very quickly and easily and may I never return to folly, on the contrary, rather let me serve You always with all my heart and to cleave to you in truth, me, together with my children and their children and all my descendants and all the seeds of Your people, the House of Israel from now on and forever. Amen, Selah.

Prayer 164

Master of the Universe, merit me to come close to genuine tzaddikim, and to stand before them to serve them and let me hear and accept with love anything they say, whether words of Torah or, seemingly mundane conversations. Whatever they say to me or command me to do, help me to behave with total faith that it is all for the good, to cure my soul. May I nullify my mind to their knowledge without a moment of doubt about them. Help me to always know and believe that they are the true curers of our souls.

Master of the Universe. I certainly believe with total belief that the Torah is the general cure for all our spiritual illnesses but I know in my soul, that I have sinned so much therefore it is difficult for me to receive my complete cure through the Torah alone. So have mercy on me and merit me to come close to true tzaddikim who are the real curers of our souls for they know how to clothe the light of the holy Torah in such a way that it will not become an elixir of death, Heaven forbid. On the contrary, my I receive from it an elixir of life to cure all my spiritual illnesses. For this reason the tzaddikim sometimes clothe the inner essence of the Torah in other simple words. And occasionally our illness is so great that we cannot tolerate even this, so they are forced to clothe the light of the holy Torah in mundane stories etc. All this acts to cure our souls. Therefore, please enable us to accept with great love anything that they say with true yearning and complete faith.

Eventually may all our Torah study turn into an elixir of life for us. Help us to study the holy Torah by day and by night. Fulfill in us the verse which says: "They are life to those who speak them out and a cure to all one's flesh".

Prayer 165

Blessed is the man whom You chastise O Lord, and teach him from Your Torah". Master of the World, Full of Compassion, who is good and does good for all, help me and save me so that I accept everything with love. Even when, in Your mercy, You sometimes send me some suffering which appears to be evil, Heaven forbid, let me merit to accept everything with really great love. Open my heart with great holiness so that I merit to really know and understand that someone like myself, as I am now, after all that I have done against You; everything that is from You is in infinitely great and immeasurable compassion and loving-kindness. It is impossible to clarify or tell of the numerous and immense mercies, loving-kindnesses and favours that You performed for me and still perform for me and which You will do for me in the future. What can I do? My transgressions have stupefied my heart and made my mind and heart so crooked that I am not worthy to feel Your love in my heart. They even want to lead my heart astray all the time, to cast doubts upon Your good attributes, Heaven forbid. Therefore I have come before You to plead that You be full of compassion towards me. Preserve me and save me from all sorts of crookedness of the heart.

Prayers from the Heart / Prayer 165

Strengthen my heart and mind in Your holy belief so as to know and believe always that You are righteous, O Lord, and Your judgments are just. In comparison to my evil and blemished deeds, You deal with me in great, immeasurable loving-kindness and mercy. In Your great mercy and loving-kindness take pity and have mercy upon me; protect me and save me from all sorts of evils and troubles and from all the suffering in the world, for You are gracious and forgive abundantly. I know that, according to my immense and numerous transgressions, all the suffering in the world would not be enough, Heaven forbid, to rectify even one sin, even the slightest of my transgressions. However, Your mercy will go before me, for You can pardon and forgive me without any suffering at all, as it says: "You have the power to forgive so that You may be feared….for with the Lord there is mercy and the power of plentiful redemption.

He will redeem Israel from all their iniquities".

Therefore Master of Compassion, I have stretched out my hands in prayer to You; have mercy upon me and preserve my soul from all sorts of evils and troubles and all sorts of suffering in the world. Don't act towards us according to our sins; don't repay us according to our iniquities. Please, Lord, You who are good and do good, make us a wonder to the living – help us and save us so that we merit to accept with truly great love all the

Prayers from the Heart / Prayer 165

suffering that You decide we need, according to Your truly merciful and kind ways. Don't send me any suffering other than when, in Your most sublime holiness, You help me to really not question Your ways at all. Let me give my soul as a guilt offering. Have mercy upon me, for Your sake. Don't let me kick against suffering but, rather, give me strength and understanding to really accept it with love when, in Your true mercy, You want to chastise me with love, as a father chastises his son and in Your bountiful mercy, ease my suffering as much as is possible, for my strength is frail and my understanding poor and I don't have strength of body or of mind to accept any suffering at all. "Grace me with your attribute of loving-kindness; with your attribute of merciful mercies, erase my sins. Enlighten me with your attribute of kindness and I will guard the testimonies of your mouth. Don't rebuke me in Your anger nor chastise me in Your fury". You who are full of mercy, make my will as You desire so that I merit to nullify my will completely in the face of Your will. Let me have no personal will at all, rather, let my will be that everything should be as You truly desire, from now on, forever. Amen, Selah.

Prayer 166 – 167

Master of the Universe, merit me to be with the true tzaddik regularly, especially when all his followers collect around him to hear from him words of the living God.

Let me receive a radiance of his holy face. May I always be counted among his followers and become part of them. Enable us to regularly come to him several times a year especially those times specially designated for his followers to gather around him. At any time when the tzaddik wants to sweeten the harsh decrees and to nullify them from upon the Jewish People, arouse then the desire and yearning of all his followers to come and collect around the tzaddik even at a time not previously designated for it. By this, the tzaddik has dominion and greater force and has the most power to nullify the harsh decrees and sweeten them.

Merit us to regularly come to the tzaddik on Shabbat several times every year. May we eat with him at his Shabbat meal. For You have told us that the days of Shabbat we spend with a tzaddik is considered like a fast-day. So help us to come close on Shabbat to the true tzaddik who is very eminent indeed and may this be considered even more beneficial in serving God than many days of fasting.

Prayer 168

Help us never to stumble by feeling proud or arrogant, Heaven forbid. Let us not have any desire or longing for status or imaginary honour. On the contrary, merit us to always run away from honour so that we will not come to any distress, Heaven forbid, as it says. "Before a fall, pride". Any honour that I receive, may it be with great holiness, only for the sake of Heaven. Fulfill in us the verse: "Before honour, humility". Amen, so may it be Your Will.

Prayer 169

Help me and save me for Your Name's Sake. Teach and instruct me how to merit to examine and judge myself, at this time of distress. I do not know how to find advice for my soul to save myself from sinning at least from now on. Until when will I (add your name) son/daughter of (add mother's name) shout out from my captivity. From where can I take advice about how to examine my deeds and judge myself regarding all my actions and traits? I know that most of my deeds are improper and very blemished. My thoughts are especially bad and confused. Heaven help me. It seems to me that I have not got myself under control. How can I merit to holy judgment, to examine carefully my thoughts and deeds in order to judge myself, by myself? Help me to find good advice at all times in such a way that I can carry it out and refrain from my bad deeds and blemished thoughts. You, Who are full of compassion, help me and save me with Your true salvation.

From where can I start? I am far away from joy, because I have blemished the brit considerably. So too the opposite. It is hard and a burden for me to repent for having blemished the brit and to rectify it, because I am very distant from happiness. The essence of guarding the brit is by means of happiness, the sages have taught us. So help me to judge myself every day about all my deeds so that I can return to You in truly complete repentance. Merit me to holy judgments so that I will judge myself as is fitting, as You desire and as the true tzaddikim desire, until I can remove and nullify all the judgments and harsh decrees from upon me. Let them not have any strength to accuse me and arouse harsh judgment against me at all. I know Master of the Universe, that I have not the strength to remove the harsh judgments by myself, so please arouse the power of the holy judgment of the true tzaddikim who engaged in judging themselves all their lives in order to remove the harsh judgments, suffering an distress from all the Jewish People. In their

Prayers from the Heart / Prayer 169

merit and their power, drive away, break, sweeten and nullify all the harsh judgments and decrees from upon me and all my family and all the Jewish People. Nullify all the troubles, generally and specifically, materially and spiritually in body, soul and money. Please do not give any strength to the 'messengers', who are instruments of the Heavenly Court, to carry out the harsh decrees against us.

We have no-one to rely upon other than You, Your compassion and Your great and holy power. Please do not look at our bad deeds. We have already suffered a lot because of them. Rather, look carefully at the little point of good that remains in us, even in the worst sinners among the Jewish People. Have mercy on the remains of Your People. Save me from all evil, from all harsh decrees in the world. Then, by the removal and nullification of all the harsh decrees, merit us to such great joy that it spreads down to our legs and we start dancing. May we rejoice in Your Salvation. Have mercy on us; strengthen us on the Festivals to rejoice with all our might. Give us the power to always be happy until we achieve a real guarding of the brit through holy joy as is fitting for a Jew who is Your Chosen People. In You bountiful compassion, guard our holy brit from all kinds of blemishes in the world, for You work wonders. Merit us very speedily to a complete rectification of the brit, as is Your desire. Help us and redeem us for Your Name's sake. Bring joy to the soul of Your servant for my soul reaches out to You.

Prayer 170

God, my God and God of my Fathers please help me to I cease sinning from now on. In Your bountiful mercy, please wipe out whatever I sinned against You, but not by our suffering or by serious illnesses. Master of the Universe, You know that we are so lowly and so weak that we do not have the strength to bare any suffering at all. Our minds are limited and very confused, especially so when we experience suffering, Heaven save us. It is even hard for us to shout and cry out to You to plead for mercy. We are inert, sleepy, tired and exhausted from the burden of the suffering. We cannot move ourselves at all.

You know the innumerable troubles and immense suffering that the true tzaddikim experience. Apart from their own great and bitter suffering they feel the distress of the Jewish People, generally and individually. But they are on such a great spiritual level that they can bear all the suffering. In addition; the greater their distress is; because of the suffering and troubles of the Jewish

People, so to their material body becomes subdued more and more. Their mind and inner essence shines more and more as their soul grows. As a result, it is almost as if they carry and lift up all of the Jewish souls, especially those close to them. They support, raise and return many Jewish souls to their source. But what can we answer after them?

The truth is that we know and believe with complete faith that all the suffering You occasionally send us, is certainly for our benefit, in order to subdue the body by crushing the materiality, so that the inner essence of the soul will grow. However, our strength is minimal, so we cannot take any suffering at all. Therefore, please have mercy on us in the merit of our Fathers and all the true tazddikim who suffered so much for our sake. Save us from now on, from all kinds of distress and suffering. Redeem us, for Your Name's sake. Amen, So may it be.

Prayer 171

Master of the Universe, merit us to come close to true tzaddikim and to hear Torah innovations from their mouths. Enable us to receive from them a new understanding in the service of God which was unknown to us until then. By this, help us to really awaken ourselves in the service of God. That is to say, from now on, may we follow the path of truth as You desire. Let us truly serve You using this new understanding that You reveal to us each time through the true tzaddikim in each generation. Protect and save us so that, Heaven forbid, we should not be an aspect of "sinners stumble in them" (words of Torah). Not only do they not serve You with this new understanding that was revealed to them, they even use it to be arrogant towards other people. So, merit us to receive all these holy understandings and to use them only for the sake of the service of God.

Prayer 172

Master of the Universe, You informed us that all the deficiencies a person has, whether in children, health or financially, are all caused by the person himself, for the light of God shines upon a person constantly. However, through a person's bad deeds he creates a shadow for himself which blocks the light and bounty of the Holy One from him. Therefore please have mercy on us and merit us to repent fully before You and improve all our deeds from now on. Help us to subdue and nullify all the materiality and coarseness of our bodies to such a degree that no worldly desire will be left in us. As a result, merit us to receive the light of God and may The honour of God be raised and aggrandized by us. Master of the World, merit us to nullify ourselves completely until we become nothing and merge with the aspect of truth. Through this, may we really receive fully the holy light of wisdom and understanding. Then let the light of God's honour shine upon us our Father. Bless us all as one in the Light of Your Countenance. Help us also, that the true tzaddikim will show us a friendly face, and through this merit us a bounty of good, a blessing and success, life, grace, loving kindness and mercy, for ourselves and all of the Israel the Jewish People. Amen, so may it be.

Prayer 173

Master of the Universe, You revealed to us that through a person's handwriting a tzaddik can know the inner essence of the soul of the writer, his faith and the source of his faith which is the inner essence of his faith. The writer puts his soul into the writing, Furthermore, the inner essence of one's soul and speech is of a greater status than that of the writing because the latter is only an expression of the soul, whereas speech is the very essence of the soul itself.

Prayers from the Heart / Prayer 173

So, have mercy upon us and merit us to minimize as much as possible our speaking and writing about mundane matters in order not to diminish the holiness of our souls and their inner essence. Rather, merit us to maximize our speaking and writing of words of Torah and words of faith for this will bring a greater radiance of holiness and faith into our souls and into the inner essence of our souls.

Help us so that even when sometimes it is necessary to talk and write about mundane matters, especially when we have to do so in the languages of the nations, that we can force ourselves to do it as much as we can without putting all our minds into it. Rather, let our souls, together with our inner souls, cleave to Your holy Torah all the time with holy faith.

Merit us to engage ourselves in studying Your holy Torah a lot, every single day while attaching ourselves to its inner holiness, which is the hidden light of Your Godliness clothed within the letters of the holy Torah. May we merit to talk a lot with true tzaddikim and hear many Torah innovations directly from their mouths of from their writings. Through this, let us merit to receive a great radiance from the light of their holy souls and their holy faith such that it will revive our souls. Amen. So may it be.

Prayers from the Heart / Prayer 175

Prayer 175

Master of the World, merit us always to be happy and to remind ourselves at all times of Your wonderful acts of loving-kindness which You perform for us all the time; And above all, that You chose us from all the nations and raised us above all their languages; You sanctified us through Your commandments and brought us close to Your service. Your great and holy Name You proclaimed upon us. So, let us be very happy with this to such a degree that we will truly regret having rebelled against You through our innumerable sins. You have bestowed loving-kindness upon us yet we have paid You back with evil. Please help us to regret this and long so much to come close to You that we are aroused to great crying which stems from tremendous joy and yearning to cleave to You. You informed us that the main perfection of crying is when it comes from great joy at knowing Your Name. Then, through this crying, enable us to sweeten all the harsh judgments and rid ourselves of sadness. Let us sweeten the harsh judgments at their source in the World Above, in Binah, which is the root of all crying and joy. Arouse great compassion upon us in the World Above, as it says, 'Behold a child was crying and she had mercy upon him.' And may it be fulfilled in us the verse 'they come crying and I will lead them back in mercy'. Amen. So may it be Your desire.

Prayer 176

"A broken depressed heart, do not reject oh God" Master of the Universe, merit us to really attach ourselves to true tzaddikim and to love them with all our soul. Then, through this may our hearts become merged with the heart of the true tzaddikim. Let our hearts become completely united with theirs until, through this all the spirit of folly that has clung to us in our heart, gets driven out. Let this spirit of folly leave our hearts with great haste so that we can achieve a really broken heart. Fulfill in us the verse which says: "God is close to those with a broken heart and saves those with a lowly spirit". So may it be Your desire.

Prayer 177

Master of the Universe, merit us to come close to true tzakkikim and Torah scholars and may we fill their throats with wine, for You taught us about the great power of the true tzaddikim and the great holiness of

Prayers from the Heart / Prayer 177

their eating and drinking. Sometimes just by drinking a little quantity of wine they merit to receive wisdom and such holy brains that, by this alone, they can achieve atonement and forgiveness for the sons of the Jewish People, as it says of Moshe: And God said, "I have forgiven, as you have asked". Merit us to guard the brit with absolute holiness such that we achieve holy brains which are perfect. Let us, take upon ourselves the yoke of the Kingdom of Heaven completely so that we nullify all our desires, to Your will. May we have no desire, other than to fulfill Your will until we become really satisfied with whatever You desire. Let us know and believe perfectly that whatever the Merciful One does is for the good, for God is good to all and has mercy over all His created beings. Merit us to raise and make greater the glory of Your Kingship through our deeds, at all times. And speedily uproot and break the kingdom of the wicked so that You throw them down and subdue them very soon, in our lifetime. Reign over us God, You alone. "May God reign forever, Your God, Zion, from generation to generation. Praise God".

Prayer 178

"**I** will greatly praise the Lord with my mouth. I will praise Him among the multitude. For He shall stand at the right hand of the poor one to save him from those who condemn his soul". Master of the World, You who greatly pardon, He who wants repentance, teach me how to praise You now, how to gladden my soul now, in such a way that I merit by happiness to confess before You and detail before You all my sins that I have committed from when I was born until this day. Thereby may I merit to truly return to You.

Master of the World, merciful Father, You know the joy wedged in my heart on one side and sadness on the other side. The greatness of the happiness and joy that I should feel as a result of my portion in life is immeasurable, beyond evaluation and beyond counting, for in Your great mercy, You granted me the merit to be born from the seed of Israel, the Chosen Nation from all the nations, and the Nation elevated above all languages.

You cherish us by all sorts of terms of endearment; You love Your people, Israel very greatly, love for ever and ever for all eternities. From Your love and compassion for Your People, Israel, You multiplied for us the learning of the Torah and the commandments,

Prayers from the Heart / Prayer 178

such that there is no end to the happiness that we have, for we should be happy and rejoice very greatly in every commandment for they give renewed strength to the soul and gladden the heart, as is written: "The statutes of the Lord are upright, gladdening the heart". However, because of the multitude of my iniquities and immense willful transgressions, sadness, worries and melancholy bear down upon me at all times, "For I will declare my iniquity; I will be sorry for my sin". You know that this sadness and melancholy does great harm to Your service, for, because of the sadness, my heart has become stupefied and my mind confused, until I cannot awaken myself to truly return to You. Even to confess before You and detail my sins and explain myself before You is very difficult and a burden, because my heart has become stupefied by the sadness and melancholy.

Therefore, I have come before You who are full of mercy, Master of happiness and joy, to ask that You have mercy upon me and teach me how to gladden my soul at all times, for, in Your great mercy, You have already taught me by the holy tzaddikim that even if a person is as he is, even if he did what he did, even so, even though he is there in the situation that he is in, he must force himself, with all his powers, to distance himself from sadness and to gladden his soul at all times, knowing that he has merited, nonetheless to be from the seed of Israel.

He must also search and desire to find in himself good points from the many good deeds that he merited to perform over the years. Every single Jew has many good deeds to his credit, for even the sinners of Israel are full of good deeds, just like a pomegranate is full of seeds. In this, it is fitting that every Jew be happy and rejoice a great deal, even the least of the least and the worst of the worst.

Master of the World, Master of Wonders, my Father, merciful Father, who might and joy is in Your place. Come to my help and save me, so that I merit to collect and gather together all the fragments of happiness from all the commandments and good points that I have merited to, from when I was born until this day. May all these fragments of happiness gather together in me, such that with great force they overcome the sadness and melancholy of my numerous iniquities, until I merit through this to be happy with all my might always. May I merit to always overcome and strengthen myself with happiness and joy by all sorts of ways of advice, which You taught me by Your holy tzaddikim.

Help me to strengthen myself with great happiness, such that I merit to dance from happiness. Let me merit

Prayers from the Heart / Prayer 178

always to the happiness of a commandment, whether it is being happy in the fulfilling of a commandment, whether at a wedding, gladdening the bridegroom and bride, or whether at other happy occasions when fulfilling commandments. Always save me and help me to have at all times great joy and happiness stemming from the happiness of a commandment, so much so that I dance a great deal because of the happiness. May I merit to be happy and dance so much that I merit to traverse the entire structure of happiness and dancing which is comprised of 248 limbs and 365 sinews, for happiness is the root of the focal point of all the 613 commandments in the Torah, as it is written: "The statutes of the Lord are upright; they gladden the heart".

In Your great mercy, let the happiness of all the truly good points that are in me from over the years be enflamed within me, in Your great loving-kindness; let the happiness shine with a great and wonderful light, such that, through this, I nullify all the darkness, obstacles, worries and sadness caused by the multiplicity of immense sins, iniquities and willful transgressions that I committed before You over the years. If they are very, very great, even so, in Your merciful eyes, virtues are considered greater and in Your great strength You can add a great light to the happiness of the commandments and good points that are in me, until they will overcome the darkness and sadness of my many iniquities and until the bad becomes nullified in relation to the good and the sadness of iniquities becomes nullified against the happiness of the commandments. May I merit always to be happy and dance a great deal through the happiness of a commandment, until I merit to really perfect happiness and to completely perfect all the structure of happiness and dancing. Through this, may I merit, in Your bountiful mercy, to judge myself truly and confess before You at all times by speaking out the specific details of my sins. May no obstacles or delay prevent me from this. May forgetfulness not overcome me, so as to cause me to forget to specify one of my sins before You. Let nothing confuse me, rather, may I just merit to truly confess before You and detail, specifically each sin. You, who are full of compassion, be ready to help me so that I merit, by confessing to build and perfect the power of speech in the way of ultimate perfection.

Through this, may the Supernal Voice join and be in complete unity with the power of speech in a way that, through this, all my sins, iniquities and wilful transgressions be rectified. May I perfect all the Names that are within Your great Name, which I spoiled.

Master of the World, Master of the World, who will give me now a mouth to speak and explain myself before You? How can I now find the strength to pour

Prayers from the Heart / Prayer 178

out my heart as water before the Countenance of the Lord? Master of the World, You, who are full of mercy – "My King and my God, I will pray to You" – teach me how to triumph over You so that You bring me to truly repent completely before You. My Father, Rock, Redeemer, Deliverer, who observes in order to better my end; help me in Your tremendous mercy, in Your great saving, in Your wonderful ways of advice, such, that I merit to always be happy. "Gladden the soul of Your servant, for to You Lord, I lift up my soul". Strengthen me and embolden me each time to overcome sadness and make happiness dominant. Strengthen me with all sorts of happiness and gladden my soul through all the paths of happiness that the holy sages taught us, in such a way that I merit always to be happy and that I not let sadness approach me in any way whatsoever; let sadness and melancholy have no strength to stupefy my heart, Heaven forbid. Let nothing confuse my mind, rather, may I merit at all times to overcome everything by great happiness and tremendous joy until I merit to speak out my confession before You with happiness and to pour out my heart before the Countenance of the Lord and to elucidate myself before You every day in a broken and contrite heart, as befits me.

Afterwards, may I immediately return to a feeling of happiness with great vigour and strength and to increase the extra happiness every time with all my might until I merit to truly repent and to serve You always, "with joyfulness and with gladness of heart, for the abundance of all things". For upon Your great, awesome, holy Name, I relied. You can help me even now to always strengthen my happiness. I will rejoice and be happy in Your saving. "I will be glad and rejoice in You; I will sing praise to Your Name, most High". Draw happiness upon us from the source of happiness, from the happiness of the future which is ready to come to us very soon through our righteous Messiah, as it is written: "For you shall go out with joy and be led forth with peace; the mountains and the hills shall break forth before you into singing and all the trees of the field shall clap their hands".

Hasten and hurry our redemption; comfort and gladden us and all Your Nation, Israel, very speedily in our days. Fulfill very speedily that which is written, "For the Lord shall comfort Zion; He will comfort all her waste places; and He will make her wilderness like Eden and her desert like the garden of the Lord; joy and gladness shall be found in it, thanksgiving and the voice of melod". Amen and Amen.

Prayer 179

Lord, God of truth, Unique and Eternal One, who thinks of ways that he who is far away (from holiness) will not be banished; who is good and does good to all; who waits for the wicked person and desires his being found righteous; who 'reads' the generations beforehand and wants repentance – have mercy upon me for Your Name's sake, for the sake of our holy forefathers, return us in perfect repentance before You. Enable me, from now on, to walk in Your statutes and keep Your commandments, forever.

Master of the World, full of mercy, who knows the hidden things; exalted and holy One "who performs mighty acts, creates new things; the Lord of wars, who sows acts of kindness and brings forth works of salvation; who creates healing; awesome in praise, Master of wonders; He, whom in His goodness, constantly renews each day, the act of Creation," and who always does very, very great and wonderful new miracles every day, which are hidden and too sublime to be understood by us, for we do not know the immensity of Your greatness and Your wonders which You perform all the time. All Your deeds, wonders and favours that You perform, all the time and at every hour, all of them, as one, are only for the true and ultimate good, which is to bring about causes so that we merit to return to You truly in complete repentance. This is the main, true ultimate good of all good. You alone know how much You create new things every day in order to bring me and all Israel back to You in true, perfect repentance; in order to purify and rectify our souls, spirits and higher souls and in order that the souls of Your Nation, Israel, become purified from their defilement. Every day, at all times, every moment, You perform completely new wonders for this purpose. No day is similar to another. Every day, at all times, every hour and every moment, You perform wonders to alter the functioning of the worlds through very many wonderful, endless changes. All this is for the good of the (people of the) world, for their true and eternal good, in order to give them innumerable signs in different aspects and ways, by which You call every individual, wherever he is at this moment, to truly draw him close to You. This alone is a really good favour; there is no other favour in the world at all apart from this.

Behold, I acknowledge and give thanks before You, my Father, my merciful Father, the good King who does good to all, for all the acts of loving-kindness, favours, salvations and wonders that You have done for me from when I was born until today. After all that has happened to me, after all that I have transgressed, by accident or deliberately by force of circumstance or willingly, after all these, Your mercy upon me has still not ceased. You still awaken me and strengthen and encourage me to wait for Your salvation and to arrange these words of mine before You. Besides this, You grant me merit every day to some awesome points of goodness which sanctify me with the holiness of Israel, with the holiness of Your awesome commandments which You give me merit to seize every day in the passing and perishable world, a world which vanishes and passes away like the blink of an eye. How great is the good You have done for me. "What shall I render to the Lord for all His favours towards me?"

Therefore, let Your servant still find in his heart the desire to plead before You, to prostrate himself in the face of Your mercy and loving-kindness. So I have come before You, Master of Compassion, Master of Salvation. "Great in counsel and mighty in deeds", that You really show me the paths of repentance. Be with me always and truly guide me every hour along the straight path, in such a way that I merit to truly return to You very quickly with complete repentance.

In Your bountiful mercy, let me merit to welcome the holy Day of Atonement in great holiness, great happiness and immense joy. May I merit to carry out all the five forms of self-denial on the Day of Atonement in absolute perfection, as is proper, and may I pray all the five prayers of the Day, in immense and awesome devotion. May I confess my sins through many forms of spoken confession, and let me regret the past completely and really leave my bad ways and evil and confusing thoughts. Let me take upon myself a very firm resolution never to return to the way of folly. Let me not do again that which is bad in Your eyes. Help me to return in complete and true repentance before You, in happiness, fear and love and let me cry a lot out of happiness.

You, who are full of compassion, let me merit to the holiness of the frightening, awesome and very sublime Day of Atonement, for it is a great, holy, awesome, frightening and mighty day. It is one day in the year that You chose for Your nation, to forgive their sins and to atone for the willful transgressions on this awesome day. Have mercy upon us and let us merit to welcome properly this great and awesome day, and to return in truly perfect repentance in such a way that You forgive, pardon and atone for us all our sins of error, iniquities and willful transgressions that are more immense, more numerous and heavier than the sands of the sea. Help us, in the merit of the essential holiness of this sacred day and in the merit of the holy fast of this awesome day, essential holiness of this sacred day and in the merit of the holy fast of this awesome day, the fast of the Day

Prayers from the Heart / Prayer 179

of Atonement, that we merit through this to subjugate all our desires to Your desire, O God, to subdue, break and nullify all sorts of desires in the face of Your desire, such that we are left with no will or craving at all against Your will. So, may we always be as You desire, never turning to the right or left of Your desire. Through this may we merit that, in Your mercy You annul the will of others in favour of our will. Annul from us all sorts of strife in the world, whether that which is between people or that which is within me: "there is no peace in my bones because of my sin". In everything that I want to do concerning holiness I have many, immense obstacles; obstacles beyond measure. The main obstacles are those of the brain and the heart. May I merit to nullify them all by the holy fast of the Day of Atonement which consists of all the days of the entire year… Have mercy upon us and let us merit to sincerely return in complete repentance throughout the entire year, especially on the holy Day of Atonement. Help us to complete the fast of the Day of Atonement with tremendous, awesome holiness and with really great happiness and joy such that, through this, I can sanctify myself from now on and know how to behave with regard to fasts during the whole year. May I really be as Your good desire is that I be, in order that I never be ashamed or disgraced or stumble.

Prayers from the Heart / Prayer 179

You, who are full of compassion, You know how many really dead and ruined days are resting in the place where they are, because of the multiplicity and immensity of my many willful transgressions that I Have committed over the years, right up to this day. You know how I extracted the life from many days with very great cruelty. It is bad enough that I did not add life from Above to these days through Torah and prayer, but I also completely extracted from them, their actual life through the many transgressions I committed in them. The rectification of these dead days is by many fasts, as You revealed to us by Your holy Sages. Have mercy upon me. Help me and save me in Your immense compassion and Your awesome and wonderful loving-kindness, so that I merit, through the power of the holy fast of the Day of Atonement and the power of all the fasts You help me to merit throughout my life, to rectify all those dead days.

Please guide us and teach us the really true path how to behave regarding fasting. You have revealed to us through the Sages the immense value of fast days and fasting which is one of the main means of repentance. On the other hand, we have been warned in the holy books not to fast without the permission of the true sage, especially when one is a Torah scholar and the fast causes one to cease studying because of weakness. But

Prayers from the Heart / Prayer 179

You, Lord our God of truth, before You, all the hidden things of the heart are revealed. You see all the doubts I have about this principally in my heart over and above all the many obstacles of the mind caused by doubts and confusions about fasting, as I mentioned previously. Therefore, I have come before You, merciful One, to ask to know how to behave regarding this on each occasion. Let me not be confused a lot by these doubts so that I do not cease even momentarily from my service. Rather grant me calmness of mind. Show me the way to behave in the matter of fasting and other areas of serving You.

May I merit to subdue and nullify my blemished desires, negating them completely to Your will. Let me attach my heart to You and Your true servants so that I swerve neither to the right or to the left from what You desire from now on and forever. Through this, please negate the wishes of others who oppose my desire to serve You. Prevent them from having any strength to disturb me or cause me to stop serving You, even for a moment. Cancel all the controversy from the world, whether from those people who wish to oppose me or whether from the controversy within my own heart. Merit me to great peace in all its aspects in such a way that I can truly repent and become as You desire from now on and for always. Then, in You great compassion, merit me to really immense happiness at all times in the service of Your Name.

In Your mercy, receive all my days with love and desire. Bring me close to You and may my soul always rejoice to such a degree that I rectify all the days I have blemished during my lifetime. Then, may I really come to You and to serve You both myself and all my descendants for all generations. He who makes peace in the Heavens, in mercy, spread peace over us and over all the Jewish People. Amen.

Prayer 180

Someone who receives redemption money should say the following prayer:

May it find favour before You that all the harsh decrees and severities be sweetened from upon (so and so son/daughter of...) by the Supreme Wonder (Pele Elion) who is great loving kindness, complete and simple mercy with no admixture of severity at all. King, Redeemer and Helper; rescuer and saviour, and sustainer and answerer and who is merciful at all times of distress and suffering; have compassion on the sick person (so and so son/daughter of...). Redeem him/her speedily from all his/her distress, from all kinds of illnesses and affliction and aches and

Prayers from the Heart / Prayer 180

pains. Sweeten and nullify all the harsh decrees from upon him/her in the merit of the money he/she gave me for his/her redemption. Have mercy upon us and consider the money that he/she gave me as if the money had reached the hands of the holy tzaddikim who know how to do the redemption and thus to sweeten and cancel all the harsh decrees by taking into their hands the money in which the severe decrees have a hold. Therefore I give over my hands and all the intentions of my heart and mind to those tzaddikim. May my actions be considered as their actions, my hands as their hands and my mouth as their mouth. And let their intentions have our good in mind so as to redeem us properly through this money which came into my hands; may they sweeten and nullify all the harsh decrees from upon (so and so son/daughter of...) in their heavenly source, in the supernal Binah.

And may the harsh decrees from This World of Asiyah be sweetened by the three hands (right, left and both clasped together) in the world of Yetzirah which add up to forty-two (three hands multiplied by fourteen joints on each hand) which correspond to the initial letters in the prayer of Rebbe Nachunia ben Hakana, 'Anna Bekoach':

Prayers from the Heart / Prayer 180

- Anna bekoach, gedulas yemincha tatir tzerora.

We beg You, with the strength of the greatness of Your right hand untie the bundle (of our sins).

- Kabel rinas amcha, sagvenu tahreinu nora

Accept the song of Your People; strengthen us, purify us o Awesome One

- Na Gibor dorshei yichudcha k'vavat shamrem

Please Strong One, those who search for Your Oneness, like the pupil of an eye, guard them.

- Barchem taharem, rachamem tzickatcha tamid gamlem

Bless them, purify them, show them mercy, may Your righteousness always reward them.

- Chasin, Kadosh b'rov tovcha nahel adatecha

Powerful Holy One with Your abundant goodness, guide Your congregation.

- Yachid Geyeh, L'amcha p'nai zochrei k'dushatecha

Unique One, Exalted One, to Your People turn, to those who proclaim Your holiness.

- Shavateinu, kabel u'shma tza'akateineu yodea talumot

Accept our screams and hear our cries knower of mysteries.

- Baruch shem k'vod malchoto l'olam va-edd

Blessed is the Name of His glorious kingdom for ever and ever.

Prayers from the Heart / Prayer 180

And in the world of Beriyah may all the harsh decrees be sweetened through the three hands which allude to the two Names of God. (Ehyeh, 21 YHV 21) that add up to forty-two. And in Atzilut they will be sweetened by the Name YHVH, in its simple four-letter form, its expanded form and its expanded expansion, which add up to forty-two. Please, have mercy Merciful One on this sick person (or this person who has another kind of distress, Heaven forbid). Arouse all the three hands in the Supernal Binah in all the Three worlds, Atzilut, Beriyah and Yetzirah. These three hands are called 'the great hand, 'the strong hand' and 'the high hand' and through this sweeten and nullify all the harsh decrees in This World of Asiyah from upon this sick person and from all the Jewish People and redeem this person quickly from all the troubles and all the harsh judgments that were decreed upon him even if it is after the decree has been sealed and send him a full cure speedily from Heaven, a spiritual cure and a physical cure, together with all sick ones of the Jewish People; and show me and teach me at all times when someone brings me money for a redemption, that I merit to know exactly how much money this person needs to give for his redemption, according to the harsh decrees that have a hold on him. Also have mercy on the person who brings the money so that he will not be miserly but rather he will give enough so that all the harsh decrees will leave him and reach and to rise to the three holy and supernal hands and let the decrees be sweetened in their heavenly source in Supernal Bina.

For it is clear and known for You that I do not know how to behave in this matter. The One full of Mercy, have compassion on this poor generation for which there is no one who can stand up for us. Have mercy on all the People of Israel, the Jewish People and on this sick person and sweeten and nullify all the harsh decrees from upon him and from upon all the Jewish People. Cure him speedily. Bring him a full recovery. Return him to his former strength and enliven him in the near future and arouse his heart to really return to You. Be full of mercy towards him for You are the Master of compassion. Redeem the Jewish People, Israel from all its troubles for we have no-one to rely on other than Our Father in Heaven, as it says: "Israel will hope to the Lord for loving kindness is with the Lord and much redemption and He will redeem the Jewish People from all its iniquities". Amen. So may it be Your will.

Prayer 184

May it be Your will, O Lord, my God and God of my fathers, that You help me to merit to attach myself and commit myself to Your service and Your fear every single day. May we merit that each individual will talk with his fellow about fear of Heaven and arouse him to Your service and Your fear, may each one remind his fellow, encourage him and inform him of Your truth and faith and greatness and goodness which fill the entire world. May the Direct Light and the Reflected Light be drawn down by us at all times and let the building of holiness be completed perfectly by us every day, every hour and at every moment. Let all the holy lights shine in our hearts in order that we really arouse ourselves to return to You wholeheartedly; let us not follow the evil cravings of the heart. Rather, let us merit all our lives to engage in learning Torah, in praying and doing good deeds. Let us add holiness and perception every single day and let every day be lengthier than the one before it, with holiness, purity, fear and love, with truth and faith, in order that we never be ashamed or disgraced until the end of time. Fulfill in us the verse which says: "Then they who feared the Lord spoke often one to another: and the Lord hearkened and heard it and a wrote a book of remembrance was written before Him for those who feared the Lord and who thought about His Name". May the words of my mouth and the meditation of my heart be pleasing before Your Countenance, O God, my Rock and Redeemer. Amen and Amen.

Prayer 185

O Lord, our God and God of our fathers, the God of Abraham, the God of Isaac, the God of Jacob, great, mighty and awesome God: May it be Your will that You have mercy upon me and bestow upon me Your holy dread, awe and fear. Guard me and save me from all sorts of 'fallen' fears, extraneous fears. Let me not be frightened or afraid of anything in this world, not from an evil animal, thieves, oppressors, or wicked people. Let me not be afraid of anything that people are usually afraid of. Protect me and save me from all of them so that I will not be afraid or frightened of them at all. Rather, let me merit, immediately and at great speed, to perceive the real truth - that they have no power to frighten or scare me other than by fear from above having fallen and it's becoming clothed in physical things. May I raise the fear to its source, so as to be in awe and dread of You and Your Presence which is terrifying and awesome: let this be, such that I merit to real holy fear and merit to raise all the fallen fears to their source, to their proper place. Raise me from level to level, higher and higher, until I merit to reach perfect, sublime fear, so that I will not have to draw fear upon myself by being aroused through lowly things into which sublime fear has fallen.

Rather, may I merit to arouse myself to perfect fear before You, such that You increase my wisdom, insight and perception with great holiness, until I achieve perfect, sublime fear through contemplation of Your greatness and grandeur; may You be blessed forever. Your fear is upon all the Angels of the Heavens, upon all those who dwell above and below. All of them tremble and are in dread before You.... You, who are full of mercy, great, mighty and awesome God, grant me really perfect fear, fear of punishment and fear of Your grandeur with the utmost, perfect holiness. Help me and save me very soon and let me merit to have the fear of You upon my face so that I will never again commit any sin or transgression at all. If I have transgressed, so let me neither return to nor add to my folly. In Your bountiful mercy, let me and my seed and all the seed of Your Nation, the House of Israel, merit to come close to tzaddikim, who are the treasury of the Fear of Heaven, for they are full of fear, awe and dread of You. Let me merit to really come close to them until I merit, through them, to receive holy and

Prayers from the Heart / Prayer 185

pure fear, lower fear and higher fear, forever higher and higher, with really total perfection. Come to my aid and save me at all times so that I can break through all the great, immense obstacles and veils that separate us and prevent our coming close to tzaddikim who really fear the Lord...

Merciful and Righteous One, mighty, awesome and fearful One. You know the immense holy fear to which the true tzaddikim merited through their worship, striving and real self-sacrifice for You, until they merited to recognize You and fear You with wonderful fear, sublime fear, higher and higher, such that there is strength in their holy fear to reach us also. Please have mercy upon us for their sake and bestow upon us something of their holy and wonderful fear such that we also will merit always to have perfect fear before You. May Your fear be upon our faces so that we never again sin. Let us return to You, truly and wholeheartedly. Have mercy upon me for Your Name's sake and let me merit to always yearn and desire to come close to real tzaddikim and those who really fear You.

May I merit, by the real craving and desire to break all sorts of obstacles in the world, to bear all sorts of hardships, efforts and suffering in order to come close to true tzaddikim; until I merit to come close to them and really cleave to them and to draw down and receive

Prayers from the Heart / Prayer 185

from them really perfect fear in such a way that I merit to be truly as You desire, forever and ever...

Master of the World, Full of Compassion, awesome and sublime – answer me! Let me merit very soon to really perfect fear. You are holy and Your Name is awesome. All the hosts of Heaven crawl and tremble in fear of Your Name. Seraphim, Chayot and the holy Opanim and all the awesome Angels tremble and are afraid of the splendour of Your Majesty. All of them perform Your will with awe and fear. Grant us fear, Merciful One; grant us fear, awesome and Fearful One. God of all the tzaddikim, who are the source of fear – grant us fear. Bestow Your awe, O Lord our God, upon all Your works and Your dread over all that You have created so that all Your works may fear You and all Your creatures may cast themselves down before You; may all form one single band to do Your will with all their heart. Master of the World, You are certainly awesome. Do awesome and wonderful things with us in such a manner that we merit to really return to You...

Holy and awesome One, save us and grant us the merit to achieve all that we have requested from You. Grant us really perfect fear of You until we merit, by this fear, to give You great satisfaction and pleasure through this and bestow upon us great bounty, blessing, compassion, life and peace, healthy children and plentiful income,

Prayers from the Heart / Prayer 185

wealth, honour and life and everything good, materially and spiritually in This World and the Next, in order that we never be ashamed or disgraced and never stumble, forever and ever. Quickly raise us higher and higher until we merit to the most perfect, sublime fear. By this, may all our deeds be perfected before You with great perfection until we merit that Your great, holy Name be perfected by us at all times with utter perfection, as is Your good will. May Your Name be extolled forever and let all the people of the world return to You and serve You with great awe, fear and fright. "Let them praise Your great and awesome Name; for it is holy". Fulfill very soon the verse which says: "God shall bless us; and all the ends of the earth will fear Him". And it says: "For the Lord, Most High is awesome, He is a great King over all the earth". May the words of my mouth and the contemplation of my heart find favour before You O Lord, my Rock and Redeemer. "Blessed be the Lord, the God and God of Israel who alone does wondrous things. And blessed be His glorious Name forever; and let the whole earth be filled with His glory". Amen and Amen.

Prayer 186

Master of the Universe, merit me to true and perfect faith in holy wise men who believe completely in the words of the true tzaddikim. Let me really believe that all their words and deeds are not simple but rather they contain mysteries and great secrets. They are full of wonders. Within their words are concealed phenomenal, wonderful and awesome innovations. May I merit to see the might of God and His wonders through the holy words of the tzaddikim. Enable us to see that everything that occurs to us throughout our lives, was alluded to in their holy words, said in truth, with wonderful sublime and awesome wisdom. All this was alluded to in their words and conversations which we heard from them or from others in their name or from their holy awesome books.

Merciful One, merit us to perfect faith, understanding and perception such that I will be able to see, in retrospect, that everything that occurred to us through Your mercy, was alluded to previously in their holy words. Merit me always to be close to and cleave to true tzaddikim and their loyal followers. May I follow in their paths of honesty and simplicity and conduct myself in these paths with perfect faith until I really return to You, as You desire.

Bring our redemption speedily, bring us the righteous Messiah. Fulfill in us the verse which says: "As in the days of leaving Egypt, let us see wonders". May the words of my mouth and the contemplations of my heart find favour before You, God my Rock and Redeemer. Blessed are You God, the God of Israel who performs wonders alone. Let the world be filled with Your glory.
Amen and Amen.

Printed in Great Britain
by Amazon